# THE APOSTOLIC SUCCESSION

# THE APOSTOLIC
# SUCCESSION

## IN THE FIRST TWO CENTURIES OF THE CHURCH

*by*

## ARNOLD EHRHARDT

WIPF & STOCK · Eugene, Oregon

Wipf and Stock Publishers
199 W 8th Ave, Suite 3
Eugene, OR 97401

The Apostolic Succession
In the First Two Centuries of the Church
By Ehrhardt, Arnold
Copyright©1953 James Clarke & Co
ISBN 13: 978-1-60608-769-5
Publication date 5/8/2009
Previously published by Lutterworth Press, 1953

# *Preface*

IT is hoped that this study will serve as a contribution
to the discussion evoked by the publication of *The Apostolic
Ministry* (1946) edited by Dr. Kirk, Bishop of Oxford. It has
been objected that the first chapters of *The Apostolic Ministry*
offer no convincing explanation for the rise of the idea of the
Apostolic succession of Christian bishops during the first two
centuries of the Church. For this reason a new and independent survey of the earliest sources of the history of the
Church has been made, in order to elucidate what meaning
the concept of an Apostolic succession may have had among
the early Fathers of the Catholic Church.

The result of this research is that the idea of priestly
succession as such is earlier than that of an Apostolic succession. It can be shown that a fairly large group of Christians
under the influence of the Judaizing Church of Jerusalem
took a strong interest in the continuation of the High
Priest's office in the new Israel, which is the Church. The
earliest lists of episcopal succession can be shown to have
been compiled with the idea of continuing the succession
list of the Jewish High Priests within the Christian Church.

This idea of a priestly succession was combined during
the course of the second century with the demand for the
maintenance of an authentic and guaranteed doctrine such
as Christ had commissioned His Apostles to preach among
all nations. In view of the dangers of Gnosticism by which
the Church was threatened during the first two centuries
of its existence, a rough-and-ready answer had to be
found which would exclude these heresies and at the same
time establish the true Christian faith. The formation of the
canon of New Testament writings had not in itself been
sufficient because of the manifold interpretations which
were available for the use of the learned heads of the various
gnostic sects. For instance, Heracleon, who based his
teachings upon St. John's Gospel, was no less dangerous

than his master Valentinus, who had referred to various
uncanonical traditions.

In this impasse the idea of an Apostolic ministry com-
mended itself in particular to the Roman Church as the
means of guaranteeing the Apostolic tradition of the
Catholic teaching. The episcopal succession to the priesthood was adduced as evidence for the purity of the Catholic
doctrine, and at the same time made dependent upon the
purity of the teaching of each bishop who claimed it.
Apostolic tradition and succession were thus joined together.
This combination appeared in the double duties of the
bishop, who as priest and as successor to the High Priests of
Israel offered the divine sacrifice and preached the Gospel
according to the traditions of the Apostles.

This combination of an Apostolic tradition and succession
fully proved its worth in the conflict between the Catholic
Church and its gnostic adversaries. It not only safeguarded
the teaching of the Apostles but also preserved the Old
Testament to the Church. The Apostolic ministry signified,
as it does to-day, that the Christian Church was indeed the
true Israel of God.

There were, however, other types of succession in the
Church. One of them, the prophetic succession, seems to
have had a certain importance in the Churches in Asia, but
it was lost during the Montanist troubles in the middle of
the second century. It left its mark, however, upon the conception of the Apostolic succession of the bishops. Another
type of succession was that of the teachers at the catechetical
school of Alexandria. This school was made subject to
episcopal authority by bishop Demetrius. His conflict with
Origen furnishes us with interesting illustrations of the
dangers arising out of the increase of episcopal authority as
a natural consequence of the idea of Apostolic succession
itself, for Origen was outspoken in his criticism of the
episcopate. He accepted the authority of bishop Demetrius
up to a certain point, but, as his demands were very high,
he found that the bishops of his time fell below his own
ideal of an Apostolic ministry.

The argument of this book may thus be summarized
briefly: the doctrine of the Apostolic succession was formed

of two elements, one being the idea of succession to the ancient priesthood of Israel, the other the idea of succession to the traditions of the Apostolic teaching. Only in so far as the former is concerned can a laying on of hands be made probable. In that sense there is reason to believe that this practice was continued in the Church of Jerusalem, and from there may have spread to other Churches. The persons who performed this ceremony were, at first, the presbyters. This privilege could hardly have been claimed by others, as neighbouring bishops were not likely to be available. If we compare the ancient traditions of Alexandria and Eusebius' report of the enthronization of Symeon as the successor of James the Just with the consecration by the Sanhedrin of the Jewish High Priest, it seems possible to provide a certain amount of evidence in support of this suggestion.

There is, therefore, sufficient evidence for the belief that the Apostolic succession of bishops can be traced back to the times of the Apostles, and in particular to the first monarchic head of the Church at Jerusalem, James, the brother of Jesus. The establishment of this belief as a doctrine belongs, however, only to the second century.

In the formulation of these findings the Rev. W. Telfer, D.D., Master of Selwyn College, Cambridge, and the Rev. Professor T. W. Manson, D.D., Rylands Professor of Biblical Exegesis in the University of Manchester, have assisted the author by their kind and wise counsel; and the Rev. G. Stephens Spinks, M.A., Ph.D., has given valuable assistance in preparing this book for publication. In thanking them all for their generous help, the author nevertheless wishes to say that the responsibility for all the statements contained herein is entirely his own.

In his learned article in the *Journal of Ecclesiastical History*, III, 1 ff., Dr. Telfer has finally demolished the theories proposed by Bishop Gore about the episcopal succession in Egypt, and the book would have benefited by the use of his results. The author can do no more than refer his readers to Dr. Telfer's results, with which he is in full agreement.

St. Clement's,

Longsight, Manchester.

*May*, 1953.

*To my dear Father in God*
THE RIGHT REVEREND
DR. G. K. A. BELL
*Lord Bishop of Chichester*

# Contents

# The New Testament Evidence

IN 1946 a volume of essays written by eleven contributors and edited by the Bishop of Oxford was published under the title of *The Apostolic Ministry*. This collection of essays attempted in an able manner to prove the uninterrupted succession of our present episcopacy. It seems, however, to the present writer that the one real gap within the Apostolic succession, that between the Apostolic and the sub-Apostolic age, has not been successfully closed by these writers. Perhaps this is due, at least in part, to the fact that the contributors have not all followed those methods now most in favour in modern historical research. For this reason this book attempts to explain, in so far as the ancient sources will allow us to draw specific conclusions, how the Apostolic succession came into being.

The new idea which the writers of *The Apostolic Ministry* have introduced is the distinction between an "essential" and a "dependent" ministry. In making this distinction they seem to have departed from the traditional doctrine of the Church by appearing to abandon the necessity for a three-fold ministry. This is the assumption which Dom Gregory Dix appears to make. It is an assumption that is not without its dangers, because it appears to be destructive of the well-established view that bishops and priests share in the sacerdotal ministry of the Church, but this seems to re-commend itself to those who are critical of the "constitutional limitations" of episcopacy. It is unfortunate that due importance is not attached to the fact that these limitations too are to be derived from the New Testament, where, in the case of the institution of St. Matthias, as well as of the ordination of the Seven, the popular vote selected the candidates, and where St. Peter had to render account before "the Apostles and brethren" of his baptizing of Cornelius the centurion.

The new theory put forward by Dr. Kirk merits careful investigation, especially as it sheds a curious light upon the change from "all bishops and curates" to "all bishops and clergy" in the intercession "for Clergy and People" in the 1928 Prayer Book. Dr. Kirk, however, is confident that his new theory will be justified by its results. To quote his own words:

> if we refuse to be dazzled by the word "bishop" (and similarly, though of much slighter importance, by the word "deacon"), and abandon the attempt to treat it as a title of order at all stages of early history, we are left, no doubt, with many gaps in our knowledge, but with few puzzles to be explained.

This statement is highly significant. It amounts to the submission that the Apostolic succession was the succession to a ministry which was "essential", but which was not from the beginning called episcopacy. It was first held by the Apostles (or by the Twelve?—the distinction between the two is not clearly defined), and after an interval by the bishops, and in between by an undefined group of "successors after the Apostles". The characteristics of this "essential" ministry, according to Dr. Kirk, are: the administration of the Sacraments, the ordination to the "dependent" ministry and the consecration of successors to the "essential" ministry. Whether the ministry of the Word is omitted by an oversight or on purpose does not appear. The "dependent" ministry, on the other hand, administers the Sacrament only by the commission of the "essential" ministry and can neither ordain nor consecrate. The ministry of the Word is once more omitted.

As regards the men who were endowed with the "dependent" ministry, we learn that their prototype is to be found in the Seven, but that Philip should be treated as an exception, because he baptized the Samaritans and the eunuch of Queen Candace at the bidding of the Holy Spirit without any commission by the Twelve. As we know so little of the ministrations of the others, except that they should "serve tables" (Acts 6 : 2), this exception of Philip seems arbitrary. Nothing is said about Ananias of Damascus, who, at the bidding of the Holy Spirit, baptized Saul, as may be inferred from Acts 9 : 18, and nothing of

the other early missionaries. Timothy and Titus too are
regarded as holding "dependent" ministries, although
Timothy was endowed with the power of laying on of hands
in general, and Titus was given the special charge "to
ordain presbyters in every city, as I have appointed thee"
(Titus 1 : 5). Also the presbyters in Derbe, Lystra, Iconium,
and Antioch in Pisidia are said to have been "dependent"
ministers, although it seems very probable that they were
concerned with the ordination of Timothy.

Regarding the "essential" ministry, there are two statements about St. James and St. Paul which deserve serious
attention. Dr. Farrer in his contribution (p. 126) claims
that St. James "inherited something of the glory of St.
James the Great", and that with him "the other brethren of
the Lord became Apostolic, according to a curious group
principle". This seems to be a very far-reaching statement.
If we believe St. Paul (1 Cor. 15 : 7), St. James had been
visited by the risen Lord, and this was what made him a
"pillar" (Gal. 2 : 9), and not his succession after St. James
the Great. For it has to be noticed that St. James the
Great nowhere appears in the first place among the
select three, but always takes the second place after St.
Peter, whereas Galatians 2: 9—unless we follow a corrupt
reading—gives to St. James the brother of Jesus the first
place. This is not sufficiently explained by his inheriting
"something of the glory" of his namesake, but only by his
actual leadership in the Church at Jerusalem, which is
plainly described by St. Luke in Acts 15. Equally hazardous
is the acceptance of Dr. Farrer's "curious group principle".
It is true that "Jude, the servant of Jesus Christ and brother
of James" is an enigmatic self-description of the author of
the Epistle of Jude, but there is no evidence from the New
Testament that he was "Apostolic", nor does Dr. Farrer's
"group principle" agree with the well-established view that
an Apostle is a man who was commissioned by a visitation
of the risen Lord to be His witness. Or are we to assume that
Andronicus and Junia (Rom. 16: 7) were "of note among the
Apostles" because they were St. Paul's kinsmen,[1] although they

---

[1] *Syngeneis* may only mean fellow Jews; cf. H. Lietzmann, *An die Roemer*,
4th ed. (1933), 125.

were "in Christ before me"? With regard to St. Paul, Dr. Kirk holds that he was an Apostle only "after his credentials had been scrutinized by his fellow Apostles". In this respect no more is needed than a verbatim quotation of the Apostle's own protest (Gal. 1: 1): "Paul an apostle not of men, neither by man, but by Jesus Christ and God the Father who raised Him from the dead." Although an attempt at defining the respective positions of the Twelve and of the other Apostles would be valuable, the approach made here seems to carry little conviction.

No names of holders of the "essential" ministry in the New Testament are given, apart from these two, and therefore, as St. James and St. Paul were themselves Apostles, it is a matter for surprise when we read that after some time "the successors of the Apostles became more and more stationary and numerous". It is not evident that there had been any such successors so far, certainly not from the New Testament, and they appear now somewhat in the fashion of *deus ex machina*. Their existence is found by way of deduction. For—to quote Dr. Kirk's own words—"the identity of function enjoyed by the second-century bishop and the first-century Apostle was too close to be regarded as a purely fortuitous coincidence". It may be asked why the New Testament should have mentioned so many holding a "dependent" ministry and yet no single one of these "successors of the Apostles"; further, the logical difficulty of a "close identity" may also cause some hesitation, because a thing cannot be more or less identical; but, passing over these minor objections, which could be multiplied, we ought perhaps to test the similarity of function between one Apostle, St. Paul, and one bishop who is representative of the second half of the second century, the one described in the Apostolic tradition of Hippolytus.

Hippolytus demanded that a bishop should be consecrated by more than one fellow bishop and to one particular see. He claimed for him the dignity of High Priest and the administration of the Sacraments, especially Holy Baptism, and the right of laying on of hands as his exclusive prerogative. St. Paul, on the other hand, "an Apostle not of men, neither by man, but by Jesus Christ", belonged to no particular see, but had "the care of all churches". He insisted that he had hardly baptized anybody at Corinth, "for Christ sent me not to baptize but to preach the Gospel" (1 Cor. 1: 17), the ministry of the Word, which we note seems already to have been almost forgotten by Hippolytus—and omitted altogether as a feature of the "essential" ministry by Dr. Kirk. Although the laying on of hands upon St. Paul at Antioch (Acts 13: 1 ff.), as will be seen, points by analogy to the separation of the tribe of Levi by a similar rite, there exists no evidence for St. Paul having claimed sacerdotal dignity. Finally, with regard to his laying on of hands upon others, the only evidence is the equivocal 2 Timothy 1: 6, as contrasted with 1 Timothy 4: 14, where it is said that Timothy was ordained by a presbytery.[1] On the whole it seems that the similarity is somewhat far-fetched, and that "close identity" is in the region of an overstatement.

It may be objected that the references are not to St. Paul and Hippolytus, but to "the first-century Apostle" and the "second-century bishop", and for these terms, although they appear to be somewhat vague, a common denominator has been suggested by Dom Gregory Dix and Dr. Kirk in the figure of the Rabbinic *shaliach*. Why the bishop should be such a *shaliach* is an open question. For *episcopos*, which, according to Hatch and Redpath's index, is found fourteen times in the Septuagint, is almost invariably the translation of a word derived from the Hebrew *paqad*, to inspect, and never of *shaliach*. It is however important to investigate the difficulties which this equation of Apostle with *shaliach* conceals. The material for this equation has been taken from Rengstorff's article *apostolos* in Kittel's *Woerterbuch*, which in its turn is dependent for its Rabbinic evidence upon Strack and Billerbeck's commentary on the New Testament from the Talmud and the Midrash. Billerbeck's remarks are intrinsically sound and deserve our fullest attention. Rengstorff, however, should be read with a considerably greater caution than that employed by Dom Gregory Dix, upon whom Dr. Kirk relies in this matter. Here are two examples:

[1] The difference between these two texts is not discussed by Dr. Farrer and only just mentioned by Dom Gregory Dix on p. 232.

The commissioning of a *shaliach* by laying on of hands, which Dom Gregory Dix (p. 228) has adopted from Rengstorff, is not found in any Rabbinic source, but has its origin in the questionable translation of *cheirotonein* in Justin, *Dial.* 108, which Rengstorff has adopted from Harnack.[1] The word means in this context—as everywhere else, where the opposite cannot be proved by complementary evidence—to commission, and not to lay on hands. Secondly, the sending out of the *shaliachs* in pairs, also adopted by Dom Gregory Dix from Rengstorff, rests only upon the evidence of one Latin inscription of the sixth century.[2] For, obviously, Rengstorff's Biblical evidence (Mark 6: 7; Matt. 16: 2; Luke 10: 1) forms the *thema probandum* and may or may not treat of *shaliachs*. The Rabbinic sources, on the other hand, make it quite clear that no sending out in pairs was contemplated.

Having disposed of these two misunderstandings, the true case for the equation between *shaliach* and apostle rests upon the fact that various Christian sources show that the Jews in the post-Christian period had apostles. The word *apostolos*, meaning messenger or even plenipotentiary, seems to have been alien to Hellenistic Greek, with the exception of the New Testament and possible occurrences in two other Jewish sources, one in the Greek Old Testament, the other in Josephus.[3] It is therefore probable that we are face to face with a specifically Jewish usage. The two Jewish in-

---

[1] A. Harnack, *Mission*, 4th ed. (1924), 1. 340. Rengstorff, *op. cit.* 1. 417, to note 69. Warning of this erroneous translation had been given already by Friedberg, *Kirchenrecht*, 4th ed. (1895), 23 n. 8. Extreme caution with regard to the equation of apostle and *shaliach* is the advice given in Cremer-Koegel, *Woerterbuch*, 12th ed. (1925), 1019, the predecessor of Kittel's *Woerterbuch*.

[2] Rengstorff, *op. cit.* n. 68. The text of the inscription, cf. A. Harnack, *op. cit.* 1. 342 n. 1, "*quei dicerunt trenus duo apostuli et duo rebbites*", from the tomb of a young Jewish woman, shows no relation to any Biblical passage. Cf. J. B. Frey, *Corp. Inscr. Jud.* 1. 438 ff. The general verdict of E. Schuerer, *Gesch. d. Jued. Volkes*, 3rd ed., 3. 44, that the inscriptions of Venosa still reflect the conditions of the imperial era, should not be stretched too far.

[3] Bishop Lightfoot, *Galatians*, 4th ed., 92 n. 3, who quotes Hesychius as saying that *apostolos* meant an admiral, and Herodotus 1. 21; 5. 38, who provides instances for the use of the word for the description of persons, suggests that this use originated from vulgar speech. J. Weiss, *Das Urchristentum* (1917) 528 n. 1, discards the testimony of Josephus, *Ant.* 17. 11. 300. Both these views are of weight, but they seem to avail little in comparison with the frequent New Testament use of *apostolos*.

stances are of a different character, for in 1 Kings 14: 6
(LXX) the word describest he prophet Ahijah of Shilo,
whereas in Josephus it seems to be used to denote a diplo-
matic envoy. In the Greek Old Testament the Hebrew word
translated is *shaluach*, which is the participle of the Hebrew
verb *shalach*, to send. This, of course, conjures up the thought
of *shaliach*. The connexion of the two is justified, but it has
to be remembered that this particular passage in the Greek
Old Testament may be of a late date. It is significant that it
does not appear in the *Codex Vaticanus*.[1] This is important,
for in spite of the various far-reaching hypotheses with which
Jewish scholars have filled the pages of their respective
journals, it cannot be proved that the word *shaliach* is found
in any Hebrew source which is earlier that A.D. 140. On the
other hand, it is evident that Jerome was familiar with the
term, for in his commentary on Galatians 1: 1, he says that
*silai* in his time was the Hebrew equivalent of apostle. I do
not know whether earlier Christian authors took notice of
the analogy or not.

The office of *shaliach* carried with it various functions. It
seems that the Jewish apostles were mainly concerned with
the taking of messages and money to and from some central
authorities, and although this was by no means their only
function—for instance, they also led the synagogue in
prayer[2]—it furnished them with a certain power of attorney;
that is, it made the *shaliach* a "proxy". Rengstorff remarks
that some form of personal representation had been introduced in the Old Testament at a fairly early time, but that
the conception reached its full maturity in the institution of
the *shaliach* only about the time of Christ. This statement
begs the question as to what limits were placed upon the
power of attorney granted in this case. The necessary
limitation of the power of attorney, even if he were acting
as a plenipotentiary, has varied in the course of legal history,
but an unlimited right to act in the name of another has
never been granted by law. Rengstorff's assertion that this
"full maturity" may be derived from John 20: 21: "as my

---

[1] It should also be considered that Symmachus in Is. 18: 2 used the word
*apostolos* to translate Hebrew *tsir*, Lightfoot, *op. cit.* 93 n. 1, so that the rendering
of *shaliach* by *apostolos* was not yet stereotyped in the second century A.D.

[2] E. Schuerer, *op. cit.* 2. 442.

Father has sent me, even so send I you" (implying that Christ imparted His full authority to His Apostles) is faulty in more than one respect. First of all, in v. 23, which follows immediately, the power imparted was limited to that of binding and loosing. For it is a well-established principle of legal interpretation that powers of attorney must be undertaken strictly in accordance with their terms of reference. Secondly, this power was given in this instance to an undefined group of disciples whom we now describe as Apostles, but who were not so described in St. John's Gospel.[1] The significance of the fact that the established body of the Twelve is not mentioned in this connexion should be emphasized. Nevertheless, Dr. Kirk translating *shaliach* as plenipotentiary, a translation which is permissible but not expressly necessary, regards the Apostles as "the plenipotentiaries of God" (p. 9) and demands that "the *shaliach*-duties of the Apostles must have been handed on . . . to the resident bishops" (p. 10). He therefore seems to see in every bishop the plenipotentiary of the Omnipotent.

This view, however, is not in agreement with a critical analysis of the facts. First, it has to be said that our evidence suggests that the term *apostolos* was earlier than the term *shaliach*. It is, therefore, hazardous to use the later term for the interpretation of the earlier. The reason for this unusual procedure as set out by Rengstorff, p. 421, is clearly insufficient. No woman, so he says, was called *apostolos*, because there was no woman *shaliach*, whereas the New Testament possesses the term *mathetria*, woman disciple.[2] This assertion is erroneous with regard to the sub-Apostolic Church; and even if it were true, it would not justify such an arbitrary use. Second, the closest similarity between the Greek and the Rabbinic terms is found where the Greek is used untechnically, as for instance in 2 Corinthians 8: 23, where the reference is to the apostles of the churches who took the money collected up to Jerusalem. In claiming a still

---

[1] The word *apostolos* occurs only once in John 13: 16, in an untechnical sense; cf. R. Bultmann, *Johannes-Evangelium* (1941) 364 n. 4.

[2] *Apostolos* does not change its ending when denoting a woman. Thus in *Acta Pauli et Theclae* Cod. G. fin. we find Thecla called *protomartys kai apostolos*. Not extant in the original Greek is Hippol., *Comm. Cant.*, ed. Bonwetsch (*T.U.* 23. 2, 1902), "Eve is called an apostle".

closer and more important parallel to John 13: 16, "the apostle is not greater than he who sent him"—still an untechnical use—Rengstorff has overlooked the fact that the Rabbinic counterpart does not have the word *shaliach*.[1] Third, the Jewish missionaries were not called *shaliachs*, as Rengstorff (p. 418) admits. If the thesis of Harnack is accepted—namely, that the statistical evidence shows that the Christian use of the word "apostle" originated among the missionary circle of St. Paul, a plausible enough suggestion considering that out of eighty-one cases of *apostolos* recorded in Bruder's Concordance seventy belong to St. Paul and St. Luke—we should conclude that the conception of *shaliach* cannot be made responsible for the introduction of the term of apostle. This does not exclude the possibility that the idea of apostle was influenced by the same Jewish customs as were eventually responsible for the formation of the conception of *shaliach*; but this conception, although it may contribute to the connotation of the term "apostle", does not touch its real essence.[3] The Jewish term *apostolos* came into existence, as Rengstorff suggests (p. 417), as a means of describing the messengers who travelled between the synagogues of the dispersion and the High Priest at Jerusalem. It may even be, as Harnack has suggested,[4] that Saul of Tarsus, when carrying letters from the High Priest to the synagogue at Damascus, was acting as one such Jewish apostle. All this points strongly to the priority of the Greek term, and it thus seems wiser to refer to the various uses of *apostellein* for the origin of *apostolos*, which Rengstorff (p. 397 ff.) has enumerated.

The discarding of the *shaliach* hypothesis is in fact of great importance for the doctrine of the Apostolic succession. Legal history shows that the power of attorney is rarely transferable. There is, of course, the current usage whereby

[1] 2 Cor. 8: 23; cf. Rengstorff, *op. cit.* 422. John 13: 16; cf. Strack-Billerbeck, 2. 558.

[2] *Mission*, 4th ed., 1. 333 ff.

[3] H. Vogelstein, *Heb. Union College Ann.* 2 (1925), 113, referring to Mark 3: 14, leaves out the crucial fact that this verse does not contain the word *apostolos*. The whole paper misses the point by not distinguishing between the general idea of personal representation through a plenipotentiary and the special institution of *shaliach*.

[4] *Mission*, 4th ed., 1. 342 n. 2, used but not quoted by Rengstorff.

the *shaliach* has the right to transfer his mandate to another person when he is acting as "proxy" for the husband at the solemn ceremony of divorce. Whether or not it is generally permitted to transfer plenipotentiary powers is, however, doubtful. We may note that in the early Rabbinic sources (consulted by Billerbeck) even the transfer of the mandate of "proxy" at a divorce was excluded. If a letter of divorce was entrusted to a *shaliach* and he was, by reason of illness, unable to deliver it, then the Jewish magistrate had the responsibility of appointing a substitute who then delivered the letter of divorce which now contained a specially conceived formula showing him to be the *shaliach* of the *shaliach*.[1] It appears therefore that even in such an extreme case the *shaliach* had no successor.[2] We are therefore forced to conclude that unless Dr. Kirk abandons Rengstorff's theory that the apostle was the *shaliach* of Christ he cannot very well maintain the doctrine of the Apostolic succession.

Under these circumstances it becomes necessary to initiate a fresh attempt designed to prove the existence of the Apostolic succession, for the Church is Apostolic with regard to its canon, its creed, and its ministry. It is not sufficient to believe that the ministry is Apostolic irrespective of any succession, solely because there existed a ministry of the Apostles in the primitive Church. An Apostle, as has been said before, is a person commissioned by a visitation of the risen Lord to witness to His resurrection, and as none of the present ministers of the Church can claim such a personal visitation, it is therefore necessary that our present witness should stand in the succession of the Apostles.

"Apostolic", therefore, may mean one of three things:

[1] Strack-Billerbeck, 3. 2 under (*b*); cf. T. W. Manson, *The Church's Ministry* (1948) 36.

[2] Vogelstein, *op. cit.* 116, is rather obscure when he says that "according to the Jewish law the *shaliach* has the privilege of naming a plenipotentiary of his own accord, a plenipotentiary who is provided with the same full authority as he himself had for the fulfilment of his legal commission or business". It is not clear what is meant by the term plenipotentiary, if the mandate of the *shaliach* was restricted to some "special legal commission or business". I am informed, however, by Dr. A. Altmann, communal Rabbi of Manchester, that the present Jewish practice has abandoned the restriction quoted from Billerbeck with regard to a letter of divorce. Vogelstein's paper, p. 115 ff., should be consulted, because it shows the differences between the position of a Jewish *shaliach* and that of the Twelve after Pentecost.

either the provenance of the ministry from one particular
Apostolic person or church; or that all the Apostles, so far
as our information goes, established and approved of it, as
an example to be followed in every church; or that only the
Twelve, as the Apostles *par excellence*, should be regarded as
its originators, be it for one particular see or for all the
churches. These three conceptions are not mutually exclusive, and may be thought of as three concentric circles.
What is suggested here is that the Apostolic succession of
bishops took its origin from the constitution of the Church
of Jerusalem, which was approved of by several Apostles as
being in conformity with the will of God, notably St. James,
St. Peter, and St. Paul. What cannot be proved is that any
of the Twelve instituted a particular succession of bishops;
or that the particular ministerial succession which, according to the Pastoral Epistles, was instituted by St. Paul has
been followed down to our own time. As a matter of fact, it
is significant for our argument that, although the Pastoral
Epistles contemplated such a succession, the tradition of the
Catholic Church contains no reference to any line of bishops
in the succession of St. Paul.

The first witness therefore to be heard is that of the New
Testament. It appears from the Acts of the Apostles that
the development of the Church constitution at Jerusalem
aroused far greater interest in Apostolic times than did the
development of Churches among the Gentiles. The Church
at Jerusalem, so it seems, proceeded from its very beginnings
along constitutional lines. After the ascension of Christ His
faithful eleven disciples regarded it as their first duty to
reconstitute the representative body of the Twelve (Acts
1: 15). The idea of reconstituting the original number of the
Twelve was proposed by St. Peter. The people addressed
upon this occasion were a group of about 120. Out of this
group two men were nominated, Joseph Barsabas, called
Justus, and St. Matthias. Then, after prayer had been made,
lots were cast and St. Matthias was added to the eleven
Apostles. It is an important feature of these proceedings that
St. Peter and the other ten Apostles played a very modest part
in the choice of Matthias. St. Peter was initially responsible
for the decision to put another disciple into the place of

Judas, but we do not hear that he even led the congregation in prayer, and so far as St. Luke's information goes the other ten were completely inactive. The nomination of the two candidates was a corporate act on the part of the whole community of believers, a community within which there were already three distinct groups in addition to the eleven—the family of Jesus, the women, and the rank and file of the disciples (Acts 1: 14). Apart from the prayer (Acts 1: 24–25), there is no mention of any further ritual and in particular no laying on of hands. Whether or not this was connected with the fact that Matthias was appointed before the day of Pentecost remains open to conjecture.

After Pentecost, when the number of Christians increased, a further appointment of Christian ministers became necessary—the institution of the Seven, commonly called deacons (Acts 6: 1 ff.).[1] In this connexion a new division of the Church at Jerusalem is mentioned, that between Hellenists and Hebrews. On this occasion the Twelve acting as a corporate body proposed the appointment of this new body of ministers and "the whole multitude" elected them, this time with a more elaborate ritual. For, after prayer had been said, the Seven were consecrated by laying on of hands (Acts 6: 6).[2] This new appointment caused the first systematic persecution of the Church by the Jews. It was directed against the Seven, and although after the martyrdom of Stephen the other six left Jerusalem, "the Apostles" remained (Acts 9: 26–27).

At a considerably later time the Church at Jerusalem once more appears in Acts as a constituted body, this time in a larger frame of a somewhat different character. As St. James the son of Zebedee was not yet executed by Herod, the number of the Twelve was still complete. St. Peter, however, when he had baptized the centurion Cornelius, was summoned "before the Apostles and the brethren that were in Judaea" to justify his action (Acts 11: 1). By this time the mission among the Samaritans had been inaugurated by Philip and regularized by St. Peter and St. John

---

[1] A. Harnack, *Kirchenverfassung* (1910) 23, is correct in saying "they were not deacons in the later sense of the word, because the diaconate was not an independent ministry".

[2] Only *Cod. D* states explicitly "by the Apostles".

(Acts 8: 14), and about the same time a mission had begun among the Gentiles at Antioch. Nevertheless, it was the intention of St. Luke to emphasize that a momentous decision had been taken by St. Peter, because Cornelius was the first uncircumcised person to be baptized. A fact significant for the constitutional history of the Church is to be found in St. Peter's justification of his action before the Church in Judaea by the explicit statement that he had followed the command of the Spirit. This may be taken as an indication that St. Peter was held accountable to an established government within the Church in Judaea, a fact which may be taken as indicative of a certain loss of status on his part.

The constitution of the Church at Jerusalem underwent a radical change after this incident. St. James the Great was martyred; St. Peter was compelled to leave Jerusalem (Acts 12), and the Twelve, who up to this time had acted as a constitutional body—under certain limitations—and held the pre-eminence at Jerusalem, were finally disrupted. How the period of "the pillars", St. James, St. Peter, and St. John (Gal. 2: 9), fits into the sequence is not clear. At any rate, at the so-called council of the Apostles (Acts 15) we find St. James in the chair and an authoritative body of "the Apostles and brethren" surrounding him (Acts 15: 6). St. Peter, having returned, is found supporting St. Paul and St. Barnabas, but it is St. James who formulates the decision. Finally, St. Paul on his return from his last missionary journey goes to see St. James, "and all the presbyters forgathered there" (Acts 21: 18). No mention is made of any of the other Apostles, and the supremacy of St. James at this juncture is self-evident.[1]

The interest of St. Luke in the constitutional development of the Church at Jerusalem provides us with a more or less coherent history of its progress, which it has been said is a deliberate attempt to disguise the violent change-over from the administration of the Twelve to that of St. James. On the other hand, St. Luke has been content to give no more than

---

[1] In Acts 21: 18 I have followed the translation of Jerome in preference to the various English versions, for reasons which will appear when the evidence of *Codex Bezae* is discussed.

occasional glimpses of the Churches among the Gentiles. His remarks about their constitutional developments, together with those found in other Apostolic writings, reveal a variety of institutions and a certain fluidity of form which seem almost chaotic. This applies first of all to the early missionaries themselves. The missionary work of the Church was begun by persons with the scantiest institutional authority. For instance, it is unknown who began the mission among the Jews at Damascus; we know no more than the fact that Christianity was firmly established there when Saul of Tarsus was sent to that city to stamp it out. It is particularly noteworthy that Ananias, who seems to have baptized St. Paul (Acts 9: 18), although he is simply described as "a disciple", required no confirmation from the Apostles for his administration of the Sacrament. This shows that it was rather the choice of the persons baptized than the authority of the person who administered baptism, which came under the scrutiny of "the Apostles and brethren". The baptism of a circumcised person like St. Paul by Ananias seems to have been nothing out of the ordinary.

At Antioch the mission among the Gentiles was inaugurated by "men from Cyrene and Cyprus" (Acts 11: 20), but who founded the Church at Antioch is unknown. The assertion in subsequent times that it was St. Peter has little to recommend it. It seems evident from the Acts of the Apostles that St. Peter did not leave Jerusalem for any length of time before the martyrdom of St. James the Great in A.D. 44, except to confirm the Samaritans, and it seems reasonably certain that the Church at Antioch was founded before that time. A similar state of affairs is reflected in St. Paul's Epistles. We do not know by whom the Romans were evangelized; but once again the tradition that it was St. Peter is untrustworthy. The relations between Epaphras, who seems to have founded the Church at Colossae, and St. Paul began only when they were both prisoners (Philem. 23). Conjectures with regard to his or anybody else's status within the Church are therefore unavailing. For instance, it is quite unknown what the *diaconia* of Archippus at Colossae (Col. 4 : 17) may have been, and on whose authority and in what way he may have been appointed to

his "ministry". Aquila and Priscilla, Apollos, and all the other
names found in the Acts and Epistles, provide a bewildering
variety of labourers in the harvest of the Lord, and we know
amazingly little of their status.

Sometimes we are met with a volume of protest against
the strictness with which the Church at Jerusalem en-
deavoured to continue the observance of the Mosaic Law.
Such is the case of Philip, who first evangelized the Samaritans, an action which might have provoked the Church of
the circumcision, had it not been that Christ Himself had
preached among them, if we may trust John 4: 39ff.[1] In any
case the step taken by Philip had to be completed by St.
Peter and St. John by the confirmation of his baptism.
Their action was designed to ensure that the gift of the
Spirit was imparted to those who had been baptized.
Nevertheless Philip was not dismayed, and at the bidding of
the Spirit, though in defiance of the rule laid down in
Deuteronomy 23 : 2, he baptized the Ethiopian eunuch,
thus making him a member of the *ecclesia* of the New Israel.
This defiant attitude is all the more important because it
excludes the possibility of his having been a Judaizer, a view
upon which E. Meyer has built some rather far-reaching
conclusions.[2] However, the missionary activities of Philip
at this period of his career took place only within the borders
of the old kingdom of David; and if later he took up his
abode at Caesarea Philippi, this may have signified no more
than that his close connexion with Stephen made it impossible for him to return to Jerusalem. On the other hand, we
find some indication of the distance between his house and
the Church at Jerusalem in the warnings given there to
St. Paul not to go to Jerusalem (Acts 21: 8 ff.).

As in the case of Samaria, so also in the case of the conversion of the Gentiles at Antioch the Church at Jerusalem
sent thither its representative in the person of St. Barnabas
(Acts 11: 22). There are, however, certain differences in

[1] If Matt. 10: 5, the advice to the Twelve "into any city of the Samaritans
enter ye not", was known to Philip, that would make his defiant attitude even
clearer.

[2] E. Meyer, *Ursprung u. Anfaenge* (1924) 3. 488, following K. Holl, *S.B.* Berlin
(1920), 920 ff. The special character of Philip's ministry was already stressed by
Eusebius, *H.E.* 2. 1. 10.

this latter case. St. Barnabas, who was not one of the Twelve, went alone. Nor did he confirm the baptisms which had been administered at Antioch. It may even be significant that in this connexion he was not described as an Apostle, although Acts 14: 14 makes it evident that he actually was an Apostle. The situation at Antioch was indeed a delicate one and demanded the presence of St. Barnabas over a considerable period. He even decided to enlist the help of St. Paul (Acts 11: 25 ff.), and after some time the two of them provided themselves with further support from Jerusalem in the person of John Mark (Acts 12: 25 ff.). The reasons for this summoning of help from outside are not known, but we hear that the result was the formation at Antioch of a body of "prophets and teachers" of whom St. Barnabas was the first, Lucius of Cyrene (probably one of the "men of Cyprus and Cyrene" who had begun the mission among the Gentiles) was the third, and St. Paul the last—a notable success for the representative of the Church at Jerusalem. It was, however, accompanied by an interesting deviation from the form of Church constitution which obtained at Jerusalem.

It may be inferred that the delicate situation at Antioch had been caused by the prophets playing a more important part than at Jerusalem, where they are just mentioned in the case of Judas and Silas (Acts 15: 32). Nevertheless, the influence of the Church at Jerusalem had beyond doubt made itself felt, and it seems wise therefore to assume that St. Barnabas and St. Paul were both influenced by the Jerusalem model when they established the constitution of those Churches which they founded among the Gentiles. This view is supported by the name which they chose for the church officers, when they appointed "presbyters" at Derbe, Lystra, Iconium, and Antioch in Pisidia (Acts 14: 23), and this suggestion may even hold good in the case of the presbyter-bishops at Ephesus (Acts 20: 17–28). The use of this title for these appointments seems to have been inspired by St. Barnabas, for it is evident from the earlier Epistles of St. Paul, as opposed to the Pastoral Epistles, that the title of "presbyter" was rare amongst the Gentile Christians. For the term is never mentioned there, only that of bishops and deacons, as for instance in Philippians 1: 1; Romans 16: 1; Ephesians 6: 21; Colossians 4: 7.

With regard to the differences between these terms, we can say only that all peculiarities of function have been obliterated. What is clear, however, is the difference in origin. The evidence collected by E. Schuerer[1] shows that in the Jewish synagogues of the dispersion the Elders were not called presbyters before the end of the third century, but rather *archontes* or *gerontes*. On the other hand, the evidence from the Gospels and Acts goes to show that "presbyter" was the only term used for the Jewish Elders in Palestine; and its popularity is stressed by the fact that the Septuagint has in two instances (Exod. 34: 30 [*Vat.*] and Josh. 7: 23) "the presbyters of Israel" instead of "the children of Israel", which is found in the Hebrew. This should be regarded as a more convincing analogy with the Christian usage than the references to Egyptian presbyters, which caused a certain amount of sensation when this term was found on certain papyri of the pre-Christian era.[2] The characteristic of the Jewish presbyters is that they almost invariably appear together with the "chief priests", a fact which also explains why they were not in existence among the synagogues of the dispersion: for the Jewish presbyters were members of the Jerusalem Sanhedrin. The significance for the Apostolic succession of this close connexion between the presbyters and the chief priests will appear in due course; for the moment it is sufficient to note the existence of Christian presbyters at Jerusalem and to relate it to Hebrews 3: 1, a passage which says that Christ had been present there as "the Apostle and High Priest".

If, therefore, the title of presbyter, when it appears in the Pastoral Epistles, provides an indication of the growing influence of the Church at Jerusalem upon the Churches among the Gentiles (*vide* 1 Tim. 5: 17 ff. and Titus 1: 5, to which 1 Pet. 5: 1 ff. and Jas. 5: 14 may be added for the sake of completeness), it should not be overlooked that a

---

[1] E. Schuerer, *Gesch. d. Jued. Volkes*, 3rd ed., 3. 39 ff.; cf. J. B. Frey, *Corp. Inscr. Jud.* 1, LXXXVII–XCI, and the index s.v. *archontes*.

[2] On the Egyptian presbyters in the temple of Soknopaiou Nesos cf. H. Hauschildt, *Z.N.W.* 4 (1903), 237. Other pagan presbyters may be found in the index of Dittenberger, *Or. Gr. Inscr.*

movement in the opposite direction is indicated by 1 Peter
2: 25. The expression used there, "the shepherd and bishop
of our souls", makes a fair bid to enlist the essentially Pauline
title of *episcopus* as the derivation of all the ministries—not
only the presbyterate—from the authority of Christ in His
capacity as High Priest; for the first person to be called
*episcopus* by the Septuagint was Eleazar, the son of Aaron,
the High Priest (Num. 4: 16). This attempt to derive the
authority of the ministry from Christ the High Priest sheds
light also upon the self-description of St. Peter as the "fellow
presbyter" (1 Pet. 5: 1); for he claimed by this title that he
was one of the entourage of the High Priest Jesus Christ—
together with those other elders who were ministering in the
Churches of Asia Minor. He thus accepted the position
which had arisen in the Church at Jerusalem, by which the
"Apostles and Elders" had been merged into one group, as
it appears from Acts 15, although it is evident from Galatians
2: 9 that, together with St. John and under the chairmanship of St. James, he had been given a special distinction.
St. Paul likewise is represented by St. Luke as having
accepted the same constitutional form at least in so far as
the Church at Jerusalem was concerned, not only at the
council of the Apostles (Acts 15), but in particular upon
the occasion of his last visit to Jerusalem (Acts 21: 18–26).
In all this the special position of St. James calls for our
fullest attention, because it was elevated above that of the
"Apostles and Elders". Its origin has been characterized by
Harnack[1] as a sort of "caliphate", since Harnack claimed that
it was founded upon St. James' family relation with Jesus.
This idea was clearly in the mind of the writer of *Codex Bezae*
(*D*), when he describes the relations between St. James and St.
Paul, but it has to be noted that the canonical Acts of the
Apostles do not provide sufficient evidence for Harnack's thesis.

It is generally conceded that St. Luke in his Acts attempted
to give a conciliatory description of the differences between
St. Paul and the Church at Jerusalem. By a study of the
variants offered by *Codex D* it is possible to see how an author
who took a partisan view in favour of the Church at Jerusalem regarded the conflict not more than a century after

[1] A. Harnack, *Kirchenverfassung* (1910) 26.

the event. We learn from Acts 15: 2 that the Church at
Antioch, the major part of which seems to have consisted of
Gentile Christians, despatched St. Paul, St. Barnabas, and
others to Jerusalem to represent their case before the
Apostles and presbyters on the question of the circumcision
of converts from the Gentiles. *Codex D*, however, reports
this matter in such a way that it appears as if St. Paul and
St. Barnabas had been summoned to appear before the
court of the Apostles and presbyters at Jerusalem by those
"certain men who came down from Judaea" (Acts 15: 1),
because they (i.e. Paul and Barnabas) were subordinate to
the Church at Jerusalem. It is also said that the same people
who had summoned them pleaded against them, and it is
significant that *Codex D*, in its version of Acts 15: 5, does not
specially mention the Apostles. It is clear that *Codex D* is
concerned to present a picture of a Christian Sanhedrin, or
rather "the" Sanhedrin of the New Israel, exercising
supreme jurisdiction over the Christian synagogues among
the Gentiles, and not of a council of the Apostles, including
St. Paul and St. Barnabas, and of the presbyters at Jerusalem. In perfect agreement with this attitude, *Codex D* calls
the decision taken there *entolai*, commandments, signifying
the authoritative, legal character of the decision.[1] The
same view prevails in the account given by *Codex D* of St.
Paul's last arrival at Jerusalem. For, whereas in the canonical
version all the presbyters forgather at the house of St. James
because of the arrival of St. Paul, the writer of *Codex D*
represents the Apostle as due to appear before them at a
meeting under the chairmanship of St. James, to render an
account to them of his stewardship (Acts 21: 18 ff.). This
difference has been obscured by current English versions,
and it is for this reason that reference has been made
previously to Jerome's translation. It is a significant difference
indeed, since it shows a diminution in the authority of the
Apostle of the Gentiles in the Jerusalem Church, and a
corresponding increase in that of the Christian Sanhedrin
and its chairman, St. James. Attempts made by F. Blass
and his followers to prove that *Codex D* exhibits the original

---

[1] The same term of *entolai* was inserted in *Codex D* in Acts 15: 41, where the
Apostles are once more omitted by the Codex itself, though not by its allies.

version of Acts have failed; but it is necessary to realize that the views expressed by the writer of *Codex D* are to be treated as evidence of the tendency which St. James had towards the strict observance of the Mosaic law, a tendency with which St. James is credited by Josephus as well as by Eusebius. We are thus confronted with a tension between the traditional views of the Christians in Judaea who demanded that the central authority should rest with the Church at Jerusalem and its leader, and the freer orders of the prophetic ministry whose authority was directly derived from their selection by the Divine Spirit of God. On a purely human level this tension may be illustrated by the warnings given to St. Paul by the prophet Agabus and by the family of Philip that he should not go up to Jerusalem (Acts 21: 10–12). These warnings show, moreover, that they had had no chance of communicating their fears for St. Paul's safety to the Church at Jerusalem in a way sufficiently urgent to cause the church authorities there to take proper precautions.[1]

If, on the one hand, the form of the court of St. James at Jerusalem reflected that of the Jewish High Priest, it is also true that it seemed to foreshadow that of a bishop in the early Catholic Church. But the Christian ministry was different from the Jewish priesthood in that it demanded a personal appointment, and was not dependent upon hereditary rights. The question thus arises: In what way was this new Christian priesthood created? And in attempting to reply we have to admit that the evidence from the New Testament on this point is somewhat limited. We may pass over the institution of Matthias, where the decision was in the end left to the lot. It is true that this method loses some of its strangeness when it is set against the Greek traditions by which the officers responsible for the administration of the sanctuaries were generally chosen by the casting of

---

[1] Cf. Origen, *Comm. Rom.* 2. 13 Lo. 6, 124, "*cuius sententiae auctoritate simul et praecepti gravitate permoti etiam post adventum Jesu suasi sunt quidam circumcidi, cum essent ex gentibus. alii vero horrescentes pondus praescripti, refugerunt penitus etiam ab ipsis legibus in quibus haec scripta videbantur, ita ut putarent haec non esse boni Dei mandata, nec eius quem Dominus et Salvator noster praedicare venisset.*" This description of the origin of Gnosticism seems to be founded upon good traditions and to describe the antithesis in the mind of the circle responsible for the readings in *Codex D*.

lots.[1] It is, however, an open question how far the election of
Matthias to the Apostolate of Judas was regarded as a
precedent in the early Church. Origen, indeed, insisted
that it was to be treated in that way, but Eusebius rightly
stressed its difference from the ordination of the Seven, and
there is no evidence that this first method was ever repeated.[2]
In contrast to the uniqueness of the institution of Matthias,
the ordination of the Seven did become the model for subsequent ordinations, particularly the ritual involving the
laying on of hands. This had been a Jewish rite, established
in the Torah, and it seems to have been continued in the
Jewish synagogues. Amongst the Jewish Rabbis it was
practised in imitation of the institution of Joshua by Moses
(Num. 27: 18, 23; Deut. 34: 9), but there are two other
instances of its use which are important for its reception
into the Church: the laying on of hands upon the Levites by
the whole congregation of Israel (Num. 8: 10) and, from
the New Testament, the case where Jesus lays His hands
upon the children (Mark 10: 16). From Hebrews 6: 2 we
learn that the laying on of hands formed a subject of instruction for the catechumens; but no trace of this has been
preserved in the New Testament, and instances of the rite
are comparatively rare. They may be divided into two
groups: the first includes the laying on of hands upon people
who in this way had their previous baptism confirmed; the
other includes the laying on of hands upon men who were
ordained for a special ministry in the Church. The first
group—which contains the confirmation of the Samaritans
by St. Peter and St. John (Acts 8: 17 ff.), and the confirmation of the disciples of St. John the Baptist by St. Paul at
Ephesus (Acts 19: 6)—although it has no immediate bearing
upon the subject in hand, should act as a warning not to
conclude that because the same rite is practised in various
places it always signifies the same thing: it is most important
to establish the intention with which it is administered.
The second group consists of the ordination of the Seven

---

[1] K. F. Herrmann, *Staats-Alt.*, 5th ed. (1884), 574 n. 7.
[2] Origen, *Comm. Jos.* 23. 2, *Werke* 7, 441, 3 ff. Eusebius, *H.E.* 2. 1. 1.
—T. W. Manson, *op. cit.* 51, strongly stresses that "in so far as the Twelve had
a special status conferred upon them by Christ, it was a personal thing and
inalienable".

(Acts 6: 6), the ordination of Timothy at the hands of a presbytery (1 Tim. 4: 14), or of St. Paul (2 Tim. 1: 6), and the dedication of St. Barnabas and St. Paul to their missionary work (Acts 13: 3). This last instance is particularly instructive, because of the information it gives regarding the pattern followed in the rite. For in Acts 13: 2 the command of the Spirit is "separate me Barnabas and Paul for the work whereunto I have called them", and in Numbers 8: 14 we read: "thus shalt thou separate the Levites from among the children of Israel".[1] It is clear therefore that in this case the model was the consecration of the Levites to the priesthood. The same seems to be probable in the case of the Seven, where the Twelve, if they laid their hands upon them, may be regarded as acting as the representatives of the twelve tribes of Israel.

In the case of Timothy the conditions were, however, rather different. When St. Barnabas and St. Paul had been sent out, an almost verbatim reference was made to the separation of the Levites, and at the ordination of the Seven a corporate act of the New Israel took place. In both these cases the idea of succession was wholly absent. Timothy, however, at his ordination received the power to ordain, through the laying on of hands, other people who, if we may follow Titus 1: 5, were to become presbyters. Moreover, the word *charisma* in 1 Timothy 4: 14 points to the gift of the Holy Spirit received by Timothy in his ordination. Both these features bear a resemblance to the ordination of Joshua, "in whom was the Spirit" and to whom Moses had given "a charge", and who "was full of the Spirit of wisdom; for Moses had laid his hands upon him". This ordination, therefore, was analogous to that practised by the Jewish Rabbis. It is of course true that the two conceptions which underlie the laying on of hands upon ministers are not mutually exclusive, and that the ordination of Joshua may have been no more than an implementation of the separation of the Levites. This view seems to find support in the fact that 1 Timothy 4: 14 appears to refer to the sending

[1] In the LXX version it is rather Num. 8: 11 which is the closest parallel. For there the Hebrew *heneph*, to hallow, is rendered by the Greek *aphorizein*, to separate, which is used in Acts 13: 2.

out of St. Barnabas and St. Paul (Acts 13: 1 ff.), and especially to the command of the Spirit in Acts 13: 2, by the words "with prophecy". On the other hand, the new conception makes itself more clearly felt in 2 Timothy 1: 6, by reason of the emphasis which is laid upon the personal relationship between St. Paul and Timothy.

With these considerations we have to approach the question as to how far the idea of a line of successors to the Apostles has found expression in the New Testament. What is absent from the New Testament is the terminology of succession. The Greeks had a technical term for succession, *diadoche*, but this word does not occur in the New Testament. *Diadochos*, the successor, is used once in Acts 24: 27 for the governor Festus as the successor of Felix, and the verb *diadechesthai*, to succeed, also occurs once in Acts 7: 45, to denote the successors of the desert generation of Israel. This shows that although St. Luke was familiar with the word he saw no reason to use it.[1] As regards the idea of succession, the words used in 2 Timothy 1: 6, "the gift of God which is in thee by the putting on of my hands", already imply its existence, especially when they are related to Moses' laying hands upon Joshua. For Joshua was clearly characterized as the successor of Moses in Deuteronomy 34: 9, and the Rabbinic tradition has used this as an example for the institution of Rabbis since the earliest times. Still more elaborate is the idea of succession contained in 1 Timothy 4: 14. First, it imparted to Timothy the privilege of laying on hands upon other men. There is just the possibility that this laying on of hands, mentioned in 1 Timothy 5: 22, was meant as a means of healing only; but the Church has never entertained this idea, and the overwhelming probability is that he received the right of ordaining and confirming. It follows therefore that his ordination, although it had been administered by a presbytery, was such as to enable him to start a succession after his own person. The second significant feature is this particular presbytery by which Timothy had been ordained. From an historical

---

[1] It is a curious fact that *diadechesthai* and its derivatives are not used in the Greek Old Testament for denoting a succession, but in the infrequent cases in which they do occur the terms mainly denote the "Second after the King".

point of view we have seen that "presbyters" had been ordained by St. Paul at Derbe, Lystra, Iconium, and Antioch in Pisidia (Acts 14: 23). As Timothy hailed from that district, it has to be assumed that it was this presbytery which was in the mind of the author of I Timothy 4: 14. If this is the case, then we are faced with the claim that the presbytery of any of the Churches from among the Gentiles possessed a right to send out missionaries similar to that by which the Church at Antioch had sent out St. Barnabas and St. Paul. This view—practically, if not intentionally—is diametrically opposed to those centralizing tendencies on the part of the Church at Jerusalem which found their expression in *Codex D*. The claim to such a privilege for all the Churches is supported by the words "with prophecy", referring, of course, to the command of the Holy Spirit. We therefore may state with confidence that in the Pastoral Epistles the attempt was made to establish a succession after St. Paul through Timothy. It is less evident, however, what sort of a succession was envisaged. The ministers who were to be ordained by Titus (Titus 1: 5) were presbyters, and therefore it is possible that the presbyters only ordained missionaries who founded new churches for which they, on their part, ordained presbyters. On the other hand, the elaborate advice about the episcopal ministry in I Timothy 3 points to the idea of an episcopal succession. There is a way out of this dilemma if the analogy of the presbyter-bishops at Ephesus (Acts 20: 17–28) is used. It seems, however, that I Timothy 3, as well as the corresponding passage in Titus 1, contemplates a form of mon-episcopacy.[1] In this case, unless we accept the view of many critics that the passages about the bishops in the Pastoral Epistles are interpolations, we have to pronounce a verdict of *non liquet* in reply to the question whether anything similar to the later idea of episcopal succession can be found in the New Testament. If I Timothy 3 and its parallel in Titus 1 are interpolations, it would seem probable that only an alternation between missionaries and presbyters was contemplated by the author of the Pastoral Epistles. In either case, such evidence as is available is derived only from the most recent writings in the New Testament.

[1] Cf. *Church Quarterly Review* (1945) 115.

## 2

## *The early Succession Lists*

INVESTIGATION of the New Testament material has
produced comparatively little evidence for the idea of an
Apostolic succession. Remarks about appointment to the
ministry and descriptions of the several ministries have
proved to be only casual, and the idea of succession, in so
far as it is found at all, is capable of more than one interpretation. Only two results are firmly established: the first, that
already in the canonical Acts of the Apostles the interest in
the constitutional development of the Church at Jerusalem
is far greater than that shown in the constitutions of the
Gentile Churches, and in *Codex D* this interest is increased to
a definite claim of primacy for St. James and his surrounding
court of presbyters; the second, that "presbyter" was a
term originating in Palestinian Jewry only, denoting the
members of the council of the High Priest, the Sanhedrin.
These results have to be kept in mind now that we turn to
the documents which are most representative of the idea of
Apostolic succession, the succession lists of the early Christian
bishops. It is the outstanding feature of these lists, as they
appear in the canon of Eusebius-Jerome, that they are
headed not by St. Peter but by St. James.

The reason for our passing over several centuries is that
it is well to define first the positions at the end as well as
those at the beginning of the historical process under consideration, before the attempt is made to explain how the
one has developed out of the other. That means working
back from the end of the fourth century when Jerome
translated the Canon of Eusebius into Latin, to the beginning of that century when Eusebius established his canon
which, alas, has come down to us only in the Latin and
Armenian translations; and beyond that to the first half of
the third century when Africanus and Hippolytus wrote

their Chronicles, which formed part of the material drawn upon by Eusebius. The research has to be continued even farther back, to the sources of Hippolytus and Africanus; and where the Christian sources fade out in the second half of the second century it will be seen that Jewish material provides supports for the bridge to span the gap of less than a century that still remains to be closed.

For Eusebius the representative succession lists were those of Jerusalem, Antioch, Alexandria, and Rome. It is true that in his *Ecclesiastical History* he refers to other sees as well, and that Tertullian[1] before him refers to Corinth, Philippi, Thessalonica, and Rome as the Apostolic sees. We know also that even before that time Hegesippus, in the middle of the second century, had taken a special interest in the succession at Corinth. However, Eusebius used only the four previously mentioned in his Canon, and founded his *Ecclesiastical History* upon them; and there exists no equally elaborate evidence of a similar age for any other Church. Even in the case of the four representative sees the evidence from Eusebius, Hippolytus, and Africanus needs careful handling. With regard to Africanus, the energetic attempt of H. Gelzer to reconstruct his work has been received with adverse criticism which has caused the Berlin Academy to postpone indefinitely the carrying out of its decision to make it the basis of an edition of that Chronicle in its series of Greek Christian writers. Although this decision was inevitable, the fact that nobody has tried to follow up the whole range of Gelzer's conclusions has imposed upon the scholar who has to use Gelzer's work a very heavy responsibility.[2] Hippolytus' *Chronicle* has been preserved in a Greek fragment of doubtful authenticity, in Latin versions, and—with many modifications—in the *Armenian Chronicle* of 686-7, all of which show mutual contradictions and discrepancies. Unfortunately, it has to be said that even the latest edition of the work, by A. Bauer and R. Helm, is far from being a final solution of the relationship between these secondary

[1] Tert., *Praescr. Haer.* 36.
[2] H. Gelzer, *Sextus Julius Africanus* (1880–86); cf. H. Sickenberger in *Pauly-Wiss.* 10. 116 ff. On the planned edition cf. E. Caspar, *Aelteste Roem. Bischofsliste* (1926) 92 n. 2.

sources. A. Bauer in particular holds strong partisan views.[1]
Finally, the Canon of Eusebius has suffered a violent revision
at the hands of Jerome. Therefore its Latin version cannot
be used without constant reference to its Armenian counterpart. Yet the Armenian is no more reliable with regard to
chronology. This state of affairs roused E. Schwartz to
deliver a most brilliant attack upon the reliability of both,
maintaining that even the Greek originals of the two versions
had been changed beyond recognition by a later revision.
Although this plea has failed to convince the majority of his
fellow historians, it has to be admitted that neither of the
two modern editors of Eusebius-Jerome's Canon, R. Helm
and J. K. Fotheringham, has succeeded in removing all
support for Schwartz's case.[2]

Under these circumstances it is convenient to give a short
exposé of the historical problems to which an answer will
be given in this chapter. The case stands as follows. In the
four succession lists which are forthcoming from the writings
of Eusebius and of the other Chronicles mentioned, the lists
of Jerusalem, Antioch, Alexandria, and Rome, the names of
the bishops, barring some few exceptions, are not in doubt.
Three things are under discussion: the periods during
which these bishops were in office, i.e. the question of dates;
the times at which these lists were compiled, i.e. the question
of age; and finally the pattern followed in these lists, i.e.
the question of their literary—and theological—origin.

On the question of dates, the point which concerns us
here is whether the early succession lists in their original
state showed the years of office of the bishops mentioned;
for the moment we are not concerned whether these dates—
or even the names—are historically correct or not. In the
Canon of Eusebius-Jerome there appears to be some uncertainty with regard to the co-ordination of the date of the
accession of a bishop with any particular year. We may note
that this Canon was divided into three main columns. On
the one side was the column of the Olympiadic years, and on

---

[1] Hippolytus, *Chronicle, Hippolytus Werke* 4 (1929).
[2] Eusebius, *Chronicle,* ed. R. Helm in *Eusebius Werke* 7 (1913–26); ed. J. K.
Fotheringham, *Eusebii Canonum,* etc. (1923); cf. R. Helm, *Abh. Berlin Akad.*
(1923), No. 4. E. Schwartz, *Kgl. Ges. d. Wiss.,* Goettingen, Abh. 40 (1895),
25 ff.; cf. *id.* in *Pauly-Wiss.* 6. 1381 ff.

the other there was a column with the names of various royal houses, giving the successive years of each king. In between these two columns, the Olympiadic calendar and the so-called *fila regnorum*, there was the so-called *spatium historicum*, mentioning events which occurred at the time and the names of the *viri illustres*. These entries were naturally not too closely connected with any particular year in those places where they referred to a certain length of time. Thus it is said of a famous poet or philosopher that he flourished at this time. It is even probable that within the *spatium historicum* special columns were provided for these period entries. Such a special column seems to have existed for the *viri illustres* and a similar one for the Christian bishops. However, the lists of the bishops show a tendency to shift from the loose system of the *viri illustres* column in Eusebius' Chronicle to the strict system of the *fila regnorum* in later Chronicles. In the lists which depend upon Eusebius-Jerome, this process found its full development in the assigning of definite dates to each single name of a bishop; but Eusebius himself was less confident. For instance, the thirty names of the bishops of Jerusalem down to Narcissus were parcelled out into four groups and assigned to four different periods. In his *Ecclesiastical History*, Eusebius made only two groups of fifteen bishops of the circumcision and fifteen bishops of the uncircumcision, and divided them by a single historical event, the destruction of Jerusalem under Hadrian. Eusebius recorded in his *Ecclesiastical History* (4. 5. 2) that in this case he was under obligation to *engrapha*, records, of the Church at Jerusalem, and the evidence seems conclusive that this list had existed there as a mere list of names, divided by this one event, independent of any other succession list of bishops or kings.

Equally conclusive is the evidence with regard to the Roman list, to be found in Irenaeus, *Adv. Haer.* 3. 3. 2, and copied by Eusebius for his *Ecclesiastical History* as well as for his Canon. In Irenaeus this is a list of names only, to which significant events from the history of the Roman Church were added. This list has been shown to be also at the root of the Liberian catalogue.[1] No co-ordination of secular

[1] E. Caspar, *Bischofsliste* 159 ff.

events was attempted, and the similarity of the Roman list with that of Jerusalem will prove to be of great importance when answering our question as to the origin of the Apostolic succession.

With regard to the lists of Antioch and Alexandria, careful research has been made by E. Caspar, who has explained the way in which the previously undated lists were—somewhat schematically—co-ordinated with the list of Olympiadic years in Eusebius' Canon. It appears that in each case an average of twelve years was allotted to each bishop. In the case of Antioch this harmonization was executed by Eusebius himself, whereas it is probable that the list of Alexandria was already arranged in that way in the *Chronicle* of Africanus and only treated by Eusebius with that amount of historical criticism which was necessary for the adaptation of a list already prepared for a chronicle similar to that which he desired to produce. In both these cases the originals had been mere lists of names, without indications of the dates of accession.[1] Caspar even gives reason for believing that Eusebius himself refrained from tying his episcopal lists too straitly to his Olympiadic calendar or to the *fila regnorum*; but preferred to indicate roughly the times of the respective bishops, a treatment similar to his method of dealing with the *viri illustres*. We therefore have to conclude that, although there existed succession lists prior to the compilation of the *Chronicle* of Africanus in A.D. 224–5, these early lists were all undated catalogues of names.

This leads us to the second question—that of the age of the succession lists themselves. This question requires a different answer for each of the four lists of Jerusalem, Antioch, Alexandria, and Rome. Beginning with the Jerusalem list, as that list is found in Eusebius, we find that it contains thirty names from St. James to Narcissus, bishop about A.D. 200. It was unknown to Hegesippus as well as to Hippolytus, but had been used already by Africanus. This brings us to the first quarter of the third century. As the list originates from the *engrapha* of the Church at Jerusalem, it is unlikely to have been a private effort. The question remains, however, whether it was compiled at the time of

[1] On Alexandria cf. E. Caspar, *op. cit.* 144 ff.; on Antioch cf. *ibid.* 133 ff.

Narcissus himself, or whether it had been built up by successive generations. We prefer the former alternative for the following reasons: First, because the list is equally divided between fifteen names of the circumcision and fifteen names of the uncircumcision, the second group being filled up by the repetition of two names.[1] Secondly, because the list of the bishops of the circumcision was unknown to Hegesippus. He had, about A.D. 150, enumerated only three of its names, St. James, Symeon, and Justus, although he too had paid special attention to the destruction of Jerusalem under Hadrian and the subsequent foundation of Aelia, A.D. 134. For these two reasons the compilation of the list of thirty names under Narcissus is virtually certain, although the material used is of a greater age.

The Roman list, appearing first in Irenaeus, was probably compiled by Hegesippus about A.D. 150. The list of Alexandria, which appears in the Canon of Eusebius-Jerome, had been used by Africanus, who had already fixed dates for each individual name. This shows that it was well established by A.D. 224–5. Therefore it was probably in existence before the end of the second century. As an hypothesis its compilation could be ascribed to the early years of bishop Demetrius (A.D. 188–9—231), during whose time of office the authority of the bishop at Alexandria rose supreme over that of the teachers. It would be too hazardous to go back to an earlier age, because of the eloquent silence of Clement of Alexandria. With regard to the Antiochene list, E. Caspar's refutation of Harnack's theory, that it was compiled by Africanus, is convincing.[2] It seems probable that it was compiled under Theophilus of Antioch, whose influence upon Irenaeus, the earliest Father who used the

---

[1] Although Eusebius, *H.E.* 5. 12. 2, says that the two names repeated, Gaius and Julianus, denote different men, we are sceptical, but are prepared to believe that they signified two separate periods of office, as in the case of Narcissus. On the other hand, this serves to show that the list was compiled in the first period of Narcissus, for if the names of the holders of the see of Jerusalem during his absence, Gaius, Germanio, and Gordius, have been omitted for party reasons, the same cannot be said with regard to Alexander, who was his coadjutor bishop during his second term of office. This consideration takes us back to the last years of the second century as the time of origin of the list.— The fact that the list is a forgery has been decisively stated by C. H. Turner, *J.T.S.* 1 (1900), 529 ff.

[2] E. Caspar, *op. cit.* 122 ff.; 123 n. 1.

Apostolic succession as an element of his theological reasoning, is well established.[1] In each of these cases, therefore, we are led to the conclusion that the authoritative succession lists arose in the second half of the second century; but it is also clear that the Jerusalem list as found in Eusebius was already an enlargement of an earlier one which had been established by Hegesippus.

The compilation of these succession lists coincided with an interesting attitude of contemporary Christianity towards the civil calendar, which was a heathen institution. A new development was seen in the tendency to fix dates which were important for the history of the Church "in the year of the Lord". This was found first in the Acts of the Martyrs, those Christian counterparts of the pagan *acta*. Of course, there was not yet available the scholarship which eventually enabled Dionysius Exiguus to co-ordinate the years of the Lord with the years of the civil calendar, but the tendency is clearly discernible. The earliest testimony for the use of *anno Domini* is the date of the Acts of Polycarp "under the everlasting kingship of Christ". The same form of dating is found in other Acts of Martyrs, notably in the *Acts of the Scillitan Martyrs*: "when they were martyred, Praesens was consul for the second time, together with Condianus; Saturninus was proconsul, and King, as we profess, our Lord Jesus Christ". In a similar manner Irenaeus dated the sojourn of Valentinus at Rome under the successive episcopate of Hyginus, Pius, and Anicetus. In these instances we observe the early stages in the formation of a new calendar. It is obvious that this was a practical necessity. The differences in the eras of the various cities and regions within the Roman Empire made the dates of the succession to any outstanding post a very important and very difficult question. The various existing lists of kings, etc., are not easy to harmonize. Their mutual temporal relations formed one of the hardest problems facing historians. These considerations provide the practical reasons for the absence of calendar dates in the early episcopal succession lists. Yet beyond these the early Christians were

[1] F. Loofs, *Dogmengesch.*, 4th ed. (1906), 146 ff.; Theophilus (*T.U.* 46. 2, 1930).

under a still greater handicap in respect of chronological research because of their belief that the judgment day was at hand. The date of *anno Domini* was first of all an anticipation of the expected end of the world. Only when this expectation was gradually fading away was the time ripe for the formation of a canon of successions which indicated the years of tenure. The original choice of a pattern for the episcopal succession lists was clearly influenced, therefore, by eschatological expectations.[1]

This question of the pattern has not yet received the attention which it deserves, although it is theologically of the highest importance. It should be obvious that the analogy of the royal succession lists is not self-evident. E. Caspar was quite right in extricating the episcopal succession lists from their entanglement with the *fila regnorum*. He has also mentioned frequently the correct analogy for the early succession lists of the Christian bishops, which is the succession list of the Jewish High Priests. Nevertheless, he has failed to realize that this pattern was in existence before the time of Eusebius, being deceived by his own erroneous translation of Eusebius' remark (*Dem. Ev.*, 8. 2. 62), εἰ δὲ χρὴ κατάλογον ἐκθέσθαι τῆς τῶν ἀρχιερέων διαδοχῆς, which means "if a catalogue of the succession of the High Priests has to be enumerated", and not "established", as Caspar translates.[2] It will be seen that it was not Eusebius who established this particular list of Jewish High Priests, and further that the alleged sources, Nehemiah, 1 Maccabees, and Josephus, were not Eusebius' sources. The words quoted clearly belong to an excerpt which Eusebius inserted in his work. Its origin will appear in the course of this chapter. This preliminary remark is meant to show only that the succession list of the Jewish High Priests was a possible pattern among the various types of succession lists; now it will be our task to show that it is the likeliest pattern, and where we must look for the development of this Jewish list.

---

[1] *Anno Domini*, cf. F. J. Doelger, *Antike u. Christentum* 3 (1932), 123, who, however, has overlooked the *Acts of Polycarp*. Irenaeus on Valentinus, *Adv. Haer.* 3. 4. 2.
[2] E. Caspar, *Bischofsliste* 100 n. 2.

It should be stressed once more that the early succession lists of Christian bishops were mere lists of names, only occasionally interrupted by references to contemporary events of Church historical importance, and that they arose in the second half of the second century. At that time there existed seven different types of succession lists all of which are available for comparison, three pagan and four Jewish. The pagan instances are the royal succession lists, the lists of periodically (mainly annually) appointed officers, and the lists of the heads of philosophical schools. The Jewish instances are the royal and sacerdotal lists on the one hand, and the prophetical and rabbinical on the other. Each of these pairs tended to fuse into one list.

It is immediately evident that the pagan lists of annually appointed officers did not serve as a pattern.[1] For there is no evidence whatsoever that any office in the Christian Church of that time ever changed hands annually. We are left, therefore, with the other two types—namely, royal and philosophical succession lists. The type of royal lists may be studied with the help of Schwartz's research in the Hellenistic lists of Eratosthenes and Castor, whilst that of the philosophical lists is found in the *prooemium* of Diogenes Laertius (10. 13 ff.) copied, as he says, from Sotion of Alexandria. We have already accepted Caspar's contention that there is no connexion between the succession lists of the Hellenistic kings and those of the Christian bishops. For, whilst the royal lists had the chief purpose of fixing the years of their several kings, the episcopal lists were originally undated. Thus the only pagan pattern which remains is the succession of the philosophers. Here, it may be argued, the Canon of Eusebius shows certain similarities between the columns of the *viri illustres* and the Christian bishops. This fact has been frequently emphasized by Caspar. However, on a general showing, Harnack's warning not

---

[1] John 11: 49; 18: 13: "Caiaphas being the High Priest of that same year", is the nearest approach. R. Bultmann, *Johannes Evangelium* (1941) 314 n. 2, has used this as an instance of John's ignorance of Jewish institutions, whereas the annual recurrences of the High Priest's duties are a sufficient explanation, even if the evidence of Eusebius' Chronicle, complaining that Herod and the Romans appointed High Priests annually and for a consideration, did not go back to very early days.

to confound the Christian Church with a philosophical sect[1] ought not to go unheeded. It should be particularly noticed that, although Caspar has stressed the similarity between the entries about the *viri illustres* and the episcopal lists, he has nevertheless built a strong case for the assumption that in the original of Eusebius' Canon these two columns were kept separate within the general *spatium historicum*. Moreover, the main purpose of Sotion in establishing the succession of the heads of the philosophical sects was the elucidation of the progress of philosophical research. No such intention can be proved for the episcopal lists, and therefore such similarities as exist are on the whole superficial.[2]

Under these circumstances the comparison between the lists of episcopal succession and one or other of the Jewish types of lists becomes necessary. With the one exception of the royal lists of the Hasmonaean dynasty, these are all undated. As the first to be tested, we select the pair of lists of the Rabbis and of the prophets. There were good reasons for compiling such lists. Already the last three pre-Hasmonaean High Priests, Menelaus, Jason, and Alcimus, had aroused very bitter feelings among the Jews against the institutional High Priesthood, and later the rule of Alexander Jannaeus became one incessant quarrel with the Pharisees, among whom rabbinical Jewry had its origin. Just as Mattathias in his speech (1 Macc. 2: 49 ff.) had mentioned (v. 54) the superlatively faithful High Priest "Phineas, our father", because he valued the connexion of his resistance movement with the official traditions of Israel, so also the Rabbis prefixed to their succession list, which is found in the first chapter of the *Pirkê Aboth*, the "Sayings of the Fathers", the name of a High Priest, Simon the Just. This was done, however, in a disguised manner. The list begins with a prehistorical part, so to speak, which contains Moses, Joshua, the Elders, the prophets, and the members of the Great Synagogue. The kings, however—even King David, who figures so prominently in the speech of Mattathias—are omitted, and the house of Aaron is also

---

[1] A. Harnack, *Mission*, 4th ed., 1. 271.

[2] On Sotion cf. Ueberweg-Praechter, *Philosophie d. Alt.*, 12th ed. (1926), 18.

absent. This part is followed by the founder of the Rabbinic succession, "Simon the Just, who was one of the last survivors of the Great Synagogue".

It is known that the High Priest Simon I was called "the Just", and he should therefore be identified with the founder of the rabbinical succession,[1] for the sacerdotal succession was the symbol of the continuity of Jewish history. The Maccabean revolution had only transferred the office of High Priest to another line of the house of Aaron, and had thus avoided a break with tradition. The Rabbis, however, were in a different position, for they abandoned the line of the blood. From this point of view the choice of Simon I was an ingenious one. First, the succession after Simon I does indeed offer certain historical difficulties. It is probable that the name of Eleazar, the alleged uncle and successor of Simon, was an interpolation in the source of Josephus, caused by his appearing in the spurious letter of Aristeas. Moreover, pseudo-Hecataeus mentions a High Priest Ezekiah as having lived under Ptolemy Lagi, slightly earlier than Simon, who does not appear in Josephus' *Jewish Antiquities*.[2] Thus it may be held that this uncertainty about the succession after Simon I accounts for his selection by the author of the rabbinical list. Secondly, the supposed successor of Simon, Eleazar, was held responsible for the translation of the Septuagint. The increasing aversion to

---

[1] For convenience' sake I have used the German translation of the *Pirkê Aboth* in A. Riessler, *Altjued. Schrifttum* (1928) 1058 ff. On the widespread suspicion of the High Priests cf. E. Meyer, *Ursprung u. Anfaenge* (1924) 2. 167 ff., referring to *Test. Levi* and other Jewish apocrypha. W. Bousset-Gressmann, *Relig. d. Judentums*, 3rd ed. (1926), 166 n. 1, rather arbitrarily reject the idea that the rabbinical succession list refers to Simon I and toy with the possibility that Simon II or III might have been called "the Just". The evidence of Josephus, however, is quite clear that "Simon the Just" was Simon I. The real difficulty is not his date but that the Rabbis did not describe him as the High Priest. If the evidence of Josephus is rejected it is much easier to assume that the Rabbis referred to some layman known as "Simon the Just". The time of the Great Synagogue, if it ever took place at all, is unknown, cf. E. Schuerer, *Gesch. d. Judentums*, 3rd ed., 2. 354 ff.; L. Finkelstein, *The Pharisees and the Men of the Great Synagogue* (1950) XI, suggests that "the Great Synagogue" had been "an authoritative body", an institution rather than a meeting, and makes it clear that Simon I was at least a century earlier than the first two heads of "the Pharisaic Order".

[2] Jos., *Adv. Apion.* 1. 22. 187; cf. E. Schuerer, *op. cit.* 1. 182 n.; E. Meyer, *op. cit.* 2. 25 n.; 28 n. 2.

this translation, especially in rabbinical circles, was sure to enhance the appropriateness of this choice.

Simon the Just is followed in the rabbinical list by the names of various rabbis which invariably appear in pairs, after Antigonus of Socho. Each of these rabbis is credited with an immortal saying, by which he is said to have enriched the great treasury of the traditional Jewish wisdom and teaching.

This type of the rabbinical list proves to be very different from that of the episcopal lists, so that it cannot serve as an analogy. It has two main features. The first is that it insists upon a succession in pairs, something which is alien to the conception of episcopal succession. The second is that the rabbinical list notes the successive generations of rabbis for their respective contributions to the store of Jewish national wisdom. Their list may therefore be compared to those of the Greek philosophers; but the Christian doctrine which maintains that the revelation in Jesus Christ is final excludes any such characterization of the bishops. For it holds that it is the task of the Apostolic ministry to administer the Divine revelation, but not to add to it. Therefore the Christian bishops were never credited in their succession lists with any such sayings, however much they themselves may have been admired for their wisdom.

The dissimilarity of the rabbinical and episcopal lists may come as a surprise. The rabbinical list, despite its good intention of avoiding a rupture, was far removed from the main current of Jewish official tradition, and it is customary to see Christianity in a similar relation to official Judaism. Therefore a closer similarity between the two might have been expected. Such a similarity in the respective positions of the Church and rabbinic Jewry is found indeed in the interest which they both took in the succession of the Jewish prophets. At an early age there existed in the Christian Church a theory of a succession of Christian prophets. The details of this succession will be discussed in a later chapter. At the moment our attention is drawn to the list of Hebrew prophets which is presupposed in the "prehistorical" part of the rabbinical list, the second type of Jewish succession lists to be examined. This list of prophets, too, arose

in an atmosphere of schism. For it is significant for the
official view at the time of its origin that 1 Maccabees
repeatedly protested that there were no true prophets,
especially at the appointment of Simon Maccabaeus to the
High Priesthood (1 Macc. 14: 41) "until there should arise
a faithful prophet".[1] Those protestations show a certain
hesitation with regard to that host of "prophetical" revelations which had sprung up since the days of Antiochus
Epiphanes, and therefore a special interest in the prophets
was probably not encouraged by the Hasmonaean dynasty.
There are, however, two lists of prophets and prophetesses
respectively to be found in the Chronicle of Hippolytus.
These lists are of Jewish origin. Such a list was in the mind
of Jesus when He referred to the prophets killed "from the
blood of Abel to the blood of Zacharias" (Luke 11: 51; cf.
Matt. 23: 34 ff.). His saying agrees well with the interest
taken in the deaths of the prophets in the collection of
"Lives of the Prophets", written shortly before His birth.
On the other hand, it explains why both Hippolytus' lists of
prophets and prophetesses finish at the time of Zechariah
the son of Berachiah, the time of the restoration of the
Temple. The Christian author completed them by his somewhat clumsy additions, *et sub Christo Simeon et Johannes
Baptista* in the case of the prophets, and in that of the
prophetesses, *et sub Christo Anna, Helisabet, Maria quae genuit
Christum.* These additions make it clear that two originally
Jewish lists were adapted for the purpose of Hippolytus'
Chronicle; but even so they cannot have been the model
for the episcopal succession lists. There are two reasons for
this: the first is that the lists of Jewish prophets were continued in the Church by a list of Christian prophets, and
it is improbable that episcopal and prophetical succession
lists should have sprung from the same root. The second is
that the Christian list of prophets included women, and
Hippolytus seems to have honoured this fact by the inclusion
of a list of Jewish prophetesses in his Chronicle. Women
were allowed equal status with the men in the prophetic

[1] Cf. also 1 Macc. 4: 46; 9: 27.—Josephus, *Adv. Apion.* 1. 40. 41, remarks
upon the lists of prophets ending with the return from the exile "because the
succession of the prophets was no longer clearly defined".

ministry—but in no other—by the Church. The fact that
Hippolytus, who was well informed about the doctrine of
the Apostolic succession, included this list of Jewish prophetesses in his Chronicle proves that the lists of prophetic succession were not connected with the episcopal succession
lists.

By elimination we have thus arrived at the result that
the combined lists of Jewish royal and sacerdotal succession
are the only type that can have been followed by the
episcopal succession lists. For proof that they actually were
the pattern, it will be shown first that such a list of sacerdotal
and royal succession was compiled before the time of Jesus
Christ; secondly, that the early Fathers of the Church were
deeply interested in that list; and thirdly, that the type of
this combined sacerdotal and royal list fully agrees with
the episcopal lists.

It has previously been pointed out how E. Caspar was
led by his erroneous translation of Eusebius, *Dem. Ev.* 8. 2. 62,
into maintaining that the succession list of the post-exilic
High Priests was first established by Eusebius. This contention has very little probability in itself, because we have the
succession list of the pre-exilic High Priests in 1 Chronicles
6: 3 ff. and the beginning of a post-exilic list in that enigmatic interpolation in Nehemiah 12: 10 ff. Nevertheless, it has
to be admitted that Caspar was deluded by a widespread
belief that Eusebius was indeed the author of such a list,
and this will be found to be true. It is, however, difficult to
see how he could ever be thought of as the author of the
first list of this kind. For it is obvious that the structure of a
complete list of Jewish High Priests is still to be found in the
tenth chapter of the twentieth book of Josephus' *Antiquities
of the Jews*. Nevertheless, Caspar was not the first historian
dealing with the various Chronicles of the Byzantine period
who neglected this evidence. It is indeed of a peculiar
character; for Josephus gives only the numbers and sometimes the first and last names of the High Priests of any one
of the periods which he mentions. Only the names of the
Hasmonaean dynasty are given in full. He says, for instance,
that twenty-eight men were High Priests from the days of
Herod to the capture of Jerusalem under Vespasian. It has

taken E. Schuerer some little trouble to compile the list
from the earlier books of the *Antiquities* and from the *Jewish
Wars* of Josephus.[1] The same will have to be done here with
regard to the fifteen High Priests who are said to have
ruled from the days of the return from Babylon to the time
of Antiochus Epiphanes. They were: Jeshua, the son of
Josedech (*Ant.* 11. 4. 75); Joiakim (*ib.* 11. 5. 121); Eliashib
(*ib.* 11. 5. 158); Joiada (*ib.* 11. 7. 297); Johanan (*ib.*);
Jaddua (*ib.* 11. 7. 306); Onias I (*ib.* 11. 8. 347); Simon I
the Just (*ib.* 12. 2. 43); Eleazar (*ib.* 12. 3. 44); Manasseh
(*ib.* 12. 4. 157); Onias II (*ib.*); Simon II (*ib.* 12. 4. 224);
Onias III (*ib.* 12. 4. 225); Jeshua (Jason) (*ib.* 12. 5. 237);
Onias IV (Menelaus) (*ib.* 12. 5. 238).[2]

The task of restoring the list of names being thus accomplished, the question may be asked whether *Antiquities* 20. 10
can be regarded as proof for the existence of a separate list
of Jewish High Priests, or whether it is to be regarded as no
more than a summary of the preceding narrative. With a
somewhat vain and superficial author like Josephus, it
seems likely that, if he had made such a list, he would have
given more than the mere numbers of the High Priests.
Moreover, we have an independent list of pre-exilic High
Priests in 1 Chronicles 6: 3 ff. and of the first post-exilic
High Priests in Nehemiah 12: 10 ff. Finally, there is a serious
discrepancy between Josephus' narrative and his list of the
Hasmonaean dynasty in *Antiquities* 20. 10, which suggests
that the latter does indeed refer to a separate succession
list. This discrepancy is found at the beginning of the
Hasmonaean dynasty. Here the list in *Antiquities* 20. 10
follows the tradition underlying 1 Maccabees—in contrast
to Josephus' narrative. From 1 Maccabees 9: 54; 10: 21, we
learn that Alcimus (Jacimus) survived Judas Maccabaeus,
who, for this reason, could not become High Priest; and
that after his death, and after an interregnum of seven
years, Jonathan was made the first Hasmonaean High
Priest. In the same sense it is said in *Antiquities* 20. 10. 237 ff.:

and Jacimus died, having held the High Priesthood for three years,
but he had no successor; but the city remained without a High Priest

---

[1] E. Schuerer, *op. cit.* 2. 216 ff.; cf. W. Bousset-Gressmann, *op. cit.* 98 n. 1.
[2] On Onias III, Jason, and Menelaus, cf. E. Meyer, *op. cit.* 2. 144 ff.

for seven years. 238. After that, however, the descendants of the sons of Asamonaeus, being entrusted with the rulership of the nation and fighting the Macedonians, made Jonathan High Priest, who ruled for seven years.

In *Antiquities* 12. 10. 413, on the other hand, the notice about the death of Alcimus (Jacimus) is followed by this remark:

414. And when he was dead, the people gave the High Priesthood to Judas.

This is afterwards taken up in 434, where it is said that at the time of his death Judas had been High Priest for three years. Still more curious is the fact that in *Antiquities* 13. 6. 212 the time of the High Priesthood of Jonathan is curtailed to four years. This leads to the conclusion that, in *Antiquities* 20. 10, Josephus referred to a list which had been in existence before his time, and to which we may put the name of Nicolaus of Damascus as its author. This list seems to have given the sum total of the years of Jonathan's High Priesthood as seven. The source of the Josephus narrative which neglected the seven years of the interregnum between Alcimus (Jacimus) and Jonathan (wishing for patriotic reasons to endow Judas Maccabaeus with the High Priesthood) could do no better than cut Jonathan's time in two and credit Judas with his first three years. It therefore appears that at the time of the Apostles there existed an elaborate list of the post-exilic High Priests, and it is likely enough that this list was also known in Christian circles.[1]

Our first question, whether there was at the time of the Apostles a complete list of the succession of Jewish High Priests after Aaron, has therefore to be answered in the affirmative. It is also evident that this list had been subjected to a revision by Jewish patriotic circles, probably among the Pharisees. The original list of the post-exilic High Priests, which is of special interest for us, was arranged in two parts. The one ending with Onias IV (Menelaus) was undated; the other, beginning with Alcimus (Jacimus) and continued by the Hasmonaean dynasty, showed the respective years of office of all the High Priests until the days of Herod, when it reverted to the earlier, undated type.

[1] E. Meyer, *op. cit.* 2. 250, has noticed the discrepancy regarding Judas, but has drawn no conclusions from it. On the general character of the Hasmonaean list valuable remarks have been contributed by E. Caspar, *op. cit.* 100 ff.; 107.

What was the reason for this deviation? It would be understandable if it had happened at the accession of the Hasmonaean dynasty; but it is different in the case of Alcimus
(Jacimus), who was regarded as a traitor. The list of
Josephus, *Antiquities* 20. 10. 237, gives him three years and,
together with ·1 Maccabees 9: 54 ff., counts seven years'
interregnum after his death. This period is fixed in 1 Maccabees as the years 153 to 160 of the Seleucid era. The
change in type would be most easily explained by the assumption that two lists, which existed independently, were
combined for the sake of completeness. It will be seen,
however, that theological considerations played their part
in this development and must be added to such a purely
mechanical explanation. These considerations, which, in
the first instance, are forthcoming from Christian historians,
will also elucidate the special interest which the list of the
post-exilic High Priests aroused in Christian circles.

The theological interest in the succession of the post-exilic
High Priests was the result of eschatological expectations.
The Christians at the end of the second century A.D., when
they began to refer to the date of *anno Domini*, and established
their episcopal succession lists, were prompted by the
same impulse. This explains the interest taken in the list of
High Priests in Eusebius' *Evangelical Demonstration*. Eusebius
neglected the list underlying the scheme in Josephus,
*Antiquities* 20. 10, for the two lists found in his works both
maintain that Judas Maccabaeus had been High Priest,
whereas the list of *Antiquities* 20. 10 does not do so. Its
author, as we believe, Nicolaus of Damascus, had been a
Gentile and had had no reason to change the evidence of
his source, the history of Jason of Cyrene, which was also
the source of our two books of the Maccabees. The two lists
of Eusebius must have come from another—later—source.
Josephus, as we have seen, knew of it, but he could not
possibly have been its inventor. For at his time the temple at
Jerusalem had been destroyed and the High Priesthood
finally abolished, so that the question of succession was no
longer of primary importance.

Jason of Cyrene was, on the other hand, responsible for
the dating of the list of the High Priests from Alcimus

(Jacimus) onwards. He made this alteration, as will be seen, for the sake of eschatological considerations. As he lived at the end of the second century B.C., these eschatological theories must have arisen some time before that. They will indeed be found to be based upon one of Daniel's prophecies. The return of the list of the High Priests to the undated type at the accession of the house of Herod was caused by the fact that the two offices of king and High Priest were no longer held by one and the same person. The Herodians claimed the dating as the prerogative of the kings, and the impulse which had caused the dating of the sacerdotal list even before Aristobulus had assumed the royal robe had lost its force by the time of the accession of Herod.

The eschatological purpose of Jason of Cyrene is shown first in 1 Maccabees 9: 54 ff., which fixes the years of the interregnum after Alcimus (Jacimus) as seven from 153 to 160 of the Seleucid era (159–152 B.C.). This was an interpretation of Daniel 9: 26: "and after three score and two weeks the unction shall fail and be no more" (LXX). This calamity was expected to last for one week, for the sixty and two weeks mentioned here have to be added to the seven previous weeks to be used for the restoration of the temple, Daniel 9: 25, and after the seventieth week there would be "sin abolished and injustice done away with", etc. (v. 24, LXX). On the other hand, the three years of government with which Alcimus was credited (Jos., *Ant.* 20. 10. 237) refer to Daniel 9: 27 (Mas.), "and in the midst of the week sacrifice and oblation shall cease". To say that the dates given are historically correct—a point of view which cannot be proved—is no argument against this eschatological interpretation of Jason's report. At best that would prove no more than that these prophecies of Daniel were contemporary. The only thing which makes the eschatological interpretation of Alcimus' three years uncertain is that it is based upon a passage the context of which is very corrupt.[1] It must not be argued, however, that

---

[1] No great store need be set by the first clause of v. 27, "and he shall confirm the covenant with many for one week". For the "he" is uncertain, the subject in *Vulg.* and *G.* being "the week", and if we accept the "he" it may yet be said that Jason thought of the Hasidean Order who accepted the High Priesthood of Alcimus.

the whole conception is too far-fetched, because this prophecy was indeed most popular. It left its mark also at
another place in Josephus' narrative (*Ant.*, 13. 11. 301),
where it is the clue to this seemingly harmless remark:

> for when their father was dead, the eldest, Aristobulus decided to
> convert his rulership into a kingship (for thus he saw fit to do), 481 years
> and three months after the people had come home from the Babylonian
> captivity.

There was no established computation of years after the
return from Babylon, and therefore this remark had a
special significance. It stated that the accession of Alexander
Jannaeus, the successor of Aristobulus, coincided with the
end of the sixty-two plus seven weeks preceding the fateful
last week before the coming of the Messiah, because Aristobulus only ruled just over one year. The Pharisaic provenance of this notice is certain because of the enmity between
Alexander and the Pharisees, and it belongs to the early
years of Alexander, because he reigned much longer than
seven years (103–77 B.C.). It is therefore not much later than
Jason and provides a valuable support for our explanation
of his intentions.

The Jewish interest in Daniel 9: 24 ff. was revived in the
theology of the Christian Church. It left its special mark
upon the Christian succession lists of the Jewish High
Priests. Two types of them are to be found, one in Eusebius'
*Demonstration* 8. 2. 65 f., and in its allies, for which the
*Excerpta Barbari* in the West and in the East the Armenian
Chronicle of A.D. 686–7 are the chief representatives; the
other in the Canon of Eusebius-Jerome, followed for instance
by the *Chronicon Paschale*. Both these types, stating that
Judas Maccabaeus had been High Priest, followed the
Pharisaic tradition, as represented by the narrative of
Josephus' *Jewish Antiquities*, and not that of Nicolaus of
Damascus and Jason of Cyrene. They were otherwise very
different in character. For the list in Eusebius' *Evangelic
Demonstration* is seriously defective with regard to the pre-
Hasmonaean High Priests, so that it contains no more than
seventeen names for the time from the return from Babylon
to the accession of Herod the Great. In the Canon of
Eusebius-Jerome, on the other hand, the full total of twenty-

one names, as mentioned in Josephus' narrative, is reached. This discrepancy tells a tale. For it shows that Eusebius indeed established a complete list of twenty-one names in his Canon, through the perusal of the narrative of Josephus' *Antiquities*, whereas in his *Evangelic Demonstration* he followed a tradition which depended neither upon Josephus nor upon 1 Maccabees.

Thus the situation at the beginning of the fourth century A.D. was as follows: the list referred to in Josephus' *Antiquities* 20. 10 was no longer in existence. Its skeleton, as preserved in this chapter, was ignored by Eusebius, who unwisely compiled the list of Jewish High Priests for his Canon from the narrative of Josephus' *Jewish Antiquities*. Unwisely, because the historical value of this source is of an inferior quality, as may be seen from the remark about the High Priesthood of Judas Maccabaeus. Nevertheless, the list in the Canon of Eusebius-Jerome is still far superior to that in his *Evangelic Demonstration* and shows clearly the marks of that admirable critical gift for which its author is justly renowned. The list in the *Evangelic Demonstration* is historically defective, yet it is from the context of this list that we learn the theological rather than historical considerations which brought all those lists into being. They sprang once more from Daniel's prophecy of the seventy weeks.

In the second chapter of the eighth book of his *Evangelic Demonstration* Eusebius offers three interpretations of Daniel 9: 24 ff., the first by Africanus, the second by an anonymous author, the third his own. In each of the three the question when to begin the period of the seventy weeks is under discussion. Africanus, rejecting the views that it should start either from the time when Daniel saw the vision or from that of Cyrus when the Jews returned from the Babylonian captivity, argued in favour of Artaxerxes I and Nehemiah, whose dates would provide the necessary number of years until the baptism of Jesus at the hands of St. John the Baptist. The anonymous author, on the other hand, produced a quite different theory. He asserted that the *Mashiach nagid*, or, as Theodotion translated it, the χριστὸς ἡγούμενος, was the catalogue of the post-exilic High Priests, beginning with Jeshua, the son of Josedech, and

ending with—Alexander Jannaeus. This period was divided
into the first seven weeks during which the reconstruction
of the Temple had taken place, and the subsequent sixty-
two weeks in preparation for the coming of the Messiah.
The strongest argument in favour of this view was that the
High Priest is called the *Mashiach* in various passages of the
Old Testament, especially in Leviticus 4: 5. Eusebius
himself, in his "third theory", discards this idea of the
χριστὸς ἡγούμενος, for he does not mention it any more,
but argues in favour of a view which would cover the time
from Darius and Ezra to the birth of Christ. Jeshua, the son
of Josedech, although he is frequently mentioned in the
Book of Ezra, could not have been alive at that time, and
his son Jozabad, mentioned in Ezra 8: 33, does not appear
in the succession list of the High Priests. The succession list
in Nehemiah 12: 10 names Joiakim as the successor of
Jeshua. It seems likely that this uncertainty caused Eusebius
to abandon the second theory.[1]

It is in the outline of the second theory that Eusebius
enumerates the list of the seventeen High Priests, which is
also found in the *Excerpta Barbari* and in the Armenian
Chronicle of A.D. 686–7, as follows: Jeshua, Joiakim,
Eliashib, Joiada, Johanan, Jadduah (these six are in
Nehemiah 12: 10 ff.), Onias I, Eleazar, Onias II, Simon,
Onias III, Judas Maccabaeus, Jonathan, Simon, Jonathan
(John Hyrcanus), Aristobulus and Alexander Jannaeus.

Obviously Eusebius cannot have been the author of this
list. The Latin and Armenian versions of his Canon agree
that it contained the complete list of twenty-one names of
post-exilic High Priests. J. K. Fotheringham and R. Helm
have shown that no drastic revision of Eusebius' Canon
took place between the death of Eusebius and the production of the two translations which are all the evidence that
we possess to-day.[2] Internal evidence, too, makes it clear
that Eusebius was the compiler of the more complete list

---

[1] The relevant passages are: *Dem. Ev.* 8. 2. 46 ff. (Africanus); *ib.* 58 (second theory); *ib.* 80 (third theory).

[2] J. K. Fotheringham, *op. cit.* XXXIII; R. Helm, in *Euseb. Werke* 7. 2 (1926), XXXIV. A. Bauer's footnotes, *Hippolytus Werke* 4 (1929), 220 ff., 514 n. 4, are off the mark, and his Alexandrian chronicle is, on the whole, an improbability.

rather than of the defective one. Moreover, the first draft of the Canon was completed in A.D. 303, and there is no reason to believe that the list of the post-exilic High Priests was a later addition. On the other hand, the later books of the *Evangelic Demonstration* were not begun before the death of Maximin Daia in A.D. 313. The list in the *Demonstration* 8. 2. 62 ff., following, as it does, upon the account given of a theory which is subsequently amended by another one, belongs very closely to the report and not to the amendment. The report itself gives the impression of a verbatim quotation, and therefore the list has to be regarded as part of it.[1]

From all this it is evident that the list of seventeen names did not belong to Eusebius but to the anonymous author whom he quoted. This leads to the further conclusion that the *Excerpta Barbari*, and the Armenian Chronicle of 686–7, did not draw upon Eusebius when they included the defective list of seventeen names, but upon his anonymous authority.[2] This conclusion has far-reaching consequences, because it makes the list of seventeen names an integral part of the theory of the χριστὸς ἡγούμενος, and reinforces the conviction derived from Eusebius' "third theory", that this theory existed before the time of Eusebius. This conviction leads us to the name of the Christian author who first adopted this theory, together with the list of seventeen names. The only Father known to have mentioned the theory of the χριστὸς ἡγούμενος previous to Eusebius is Hippolytus,[3] and it is a recognized fact that both the *Excerpta Barbari* and the Armenian Chronicle of 686–7 are in many respects dependent upon his Chronicle. Africanus, the other possible source, is excluded because it is evident from his remark which precedes the theory of the

---

[1] On the date of Euseb., *Dem. Ev.*, cf. A. Harnack, *Chronologie* 2. 2 (1904), 120.

[2] The praise given to Eusebius by E. Schwartz, *Koenigslisten*, 29 n. 1, is therefore undeserved.

[3] Hippol., *Comm. Dan.* 4. 30. 6. E. Caspar, *op. cit.* 97 n. 2, may be mistaken in assuming that another reference is found in Clem. Alex., *Strom.* 1. 126. 1, "that the temple was built in seven weeks is clear, for Ezra says so; and thus the χριστὸς ἡγούμευος became king of the Jews, after the completion of the seven weeks, at Jerusalem". Note, on the other hand, that in the Zadokite work 9. 29 (Riessler), cf. *ib.* 15. 4, the Messiah is expected "out of Aaron and Israel", which seems to be the starting-point of the χριστὸς ἡγούμενος theory.

χριστὸς ἡγούμενος that he began the period of the sixty-nine weeks only with Artaxerxes and Nehemiah, which excludes the catalogue of post-exilic High Priests from playing a part in his considerations. For although the dates in Eusebius' "third theory" might perhaps be stretched so far as to allow the first post-exilic High Priest, Jeshua, the son of Josedech, to have been still alive under Darius, it would seem impossible that he should have lived on into the days of Artaxerxes. Eusebius did not mention the name of Hippolytus, because he was a schismatic. The *Ecclesiastical History* 6. 46. 5 makes it plain that Eusebius knew of his schism from the "diaconic" epistle of Pope Dionysius of Alexandria.[1]

Hippolytus can also be shown to be the author of the "second theory" by its close resemblance to Pseudo-Hegesippus 2. 13. 1. The literal identity of their remarks about Aristobulus and Alexander Jannaeus may illustrate their interdependence:

> after him Aristobulus ruled one year, the first who after the return from Babylon took the royal diadem together with the High Priesthood.

---

[1] The only serious objection to this conclusion may come from the defective lists of post-exilic High Priests in the two *Libri Generationis*, now generally accepted as first-hand evidence for Hippolytus' Chronicle. However, the original had no such list in this context, for: (a) Pseudo-Hegesippus, the other first-hand evidence, omits it; (b) the *Liber Generationis* II, the older of the two, proves unreliable in that it leaves out the name of Josedech, maintaining that Jeshua, who returned from the Babylonian exile, was the immediate successor of Sareas (Seraiah, 1 Chron. 6: 14); (c) three of the four or five names given as post-exilic High Priests in the *Libri Generationis* can be shown to have arisen out of corruptions or interpolations. There is the first successor of Jeshua, the son of Josedech, named Helcias, together with his son Joachim. These two really lived under King Hezekiah, 2 Kings 18: 18; Is. 22: 20. Only in view of the promise of Isaiah that Eliakim—that is the name given by him—should be High Priest, a promise which is not fulfilled in the official list, 1 Chron. 6: 13, have these names been put here, probably from a marginal note in the original Chronicle of Hippolytus by its Latin translator. The name of Zacharias, on the other hand, is probably that of the father of John the Baptist, which the author of the *Liber Generationis* II had added on his own account, for it is left out in the *Liber Generationis* I, which is a revised edition of the former. Thus there remains only one name, that of Zadok, to be accounted for. Although it is not evident to whom this name may refer, it would be difficult to maintain that it is sufficient proof for a continuation of the list of High Priests in this context, beyond the time of the exile. The post-exilic list had its place somewhere else in Hippolytus' Chronicle. The reason for this assumption is that the whole quotation in Eusebius' *Evangelic Demonstration* was part of that work, and such an elaborate statement had to be given a place of its own.

57

74. He was followed by Alexander, both king and High Priest, who ruled supreme for twenty seven years. (*Dem. Ev.* 8. 2. 73.)

*Hyrcano autem Aristobolus qui etiam regnum memorato adiunxit muneri, ut utriusque esset particeps; et Aristobolo Alexander substituti sunt. Penes Alexandrum et regnum et sacerdotium usque ad diem vitae eius mansit supremum, per septem et viginti annos.* (*Ps. Hegesipp.*, 2. 13. 1.)

The importance of Pseudo-Hegesippus for the restitution of Hippolytus' Chronicle is frequently emphasized in A. Bauer's edition, and this close resemblance of the two texts is sufficient evidence for attributing both to this source. In view of this similarity it is surprising to find that Pseudo-Hegesippus 2. 13. 1 begins as a translation of Josephus, *Antiquities* 20. 10. 238 ff., and that the similarity to this source is still discernible in the two passages quoted, although it is slightly more remote. For the list in the *Demonstration* 8. 2. 62 ff. includes the name of Judas Maccabaeus, and is therefore far removed from *Antiquities* 20. 10. More curious still is the fact that the three allies part company immediately after the passage quoted. The "second theory" embarks upon the doctrine of the χριστὸς ἡγούμενος, but this, as Schwartz[1] has rightly remarked, was never accepted by the Church. Pseudo-Hegesippus, therefore, has a non-committal remark about the unpopularity of Alexander Jannaeus. Finally, *Antiquities* 20. 10 continues with its list of High Priests. However, the first two join forces again immediately afterwards, but their remarks betray a complete independence of anything resembling a list of High Priests. They amount to a lengthy description of the fate of Queen Salome (Alexandra) and her two sons, ending with the desecration of the Temple by Pompey. The reason for this apparent break is to be found in the influence of a source related to but not identical with Josephus.

Jewish theology had been busily occupied to find the date of the last of the seventy weeks prophesied by Daniel. The earliest computation led to the time of Antiochus Epiphanes. This is shown by the report in 1 Maccabees 1: 57, saying that under this king the abomination of desolation was placed upon God's altar. For the term "abomination of desolation", which also occurs in Daniel 11: 31, took its

[1] *Koenigslisten* 29 n. 1.

origin from the prophecy in Daniel 9: 27 (LXX and Theod.),
"abomination of desolations" 1 Maccabees 1: 57, therefore,
exhibits a clear reference to Daniel's prophecy about
the seventy weeks. When the prophecy failed to be fulfilled
at that time, the second step was that Jason of Cyrene found
reasons, as we have seen, to move the time to the rule of
the traitor Alcimus (Jacimus), regarding the seven years
after the death of the traitor during which the throne of the
High Priest was vacant as the last of Daniel's seventy weeks.
The third step was taken by the source accepted as authoritative by Josephus (*Ant.* 13. 11. 301), probably of Pharisaic
origin. It vented its animosity against Alexander Jannaeus,
claiming that his accession coincided with the last week of
Daniel's prophecy. This source was behind the χριστὸς
ἡγούμενος-theory. When that prophecy also failed to
materialize, the catastrophe of the Temple under Pompey
and remarks about Herod were added in a revision of the
source, but its chronology was not altered. All this was
faithfully copied by Hippolytus, whereas Africanus and
Eusebius, both of whom had a passion for chronology,
devised new systems. We find therefore that the episcopal
succession lists not only followed the pattern of the Jewish
lists of High Priests, but that an early father, like Hippolytus
of Rome, even adopted the special theological point of
view, under which the post-exilic list had found its exceptional importance in pre-Christian Judaism.

It is tempting to combine the early description of the
bishops as High Priests with this copying of the pattern of
the succession list of the Jewish High Priests. For this
purpose a purely hypothetical explanation of a somewhat
puzzling coincidence has been added here, which suggests
an interdependence between the episcopal lists of Jerusalem
and Rome on the one hand, and of the post-exilic High
Priests until Jesus (Jason) on the other, in a way which is
characteristic of the mind of that time. In the skeleton list
(*Ant.* 20. 10), the number of these post-exilic High Priests
was given as fifteen. The number of bishops of the circumcision at Jerusalem, prior to the destruction of the city
under Hadrian, was also fifteen. The same number of bishops
of the uncircumcision at Jerusalem prompted that Church

under bishop Narcissus to compile its revised succession list. Moreover, the first bishop of Rome whose date was historically fixed, Pope Callistus, was the sixteenth in the list, if the name of St. Peter is included. This coincidence suggests the influence of the earlier list upon those three later ones. We know from Pseudo-Hegesippus that attention was paid to the skeleton list in *Antiquities* 20. 10 by the Church of Rome much later than the time of Callistus, and it is tempting to surmise that Hippolytus in his Chronicle intentionally changed over to his defective list of seventeen post-exilic High Priests, in order to confound the analogy which was claimed by his adversary Callistus.

Our research into the early succession lists of bishops has therefore produced the following results. First of all, it has proved that these lists were compiled in the second half of the second century, and it has therefore fixed the time from which we shall have to start working back to the New Testament period. Secondly, it has proved that the early episcopal succession lists were mere lists of names, occasionally, but not very frequently, referring to events of Church historical importance. The main interest of their compilers centred in the fact that the sees were occupied without interruption, but not in the dates of accession of their respective holders. The break at Jerusalem was registered for this reason. This question of dates was linked up with the introduction of the idea of *anno Domini*, which was boldly opposed to the pagan civil calendar. This idea, although it became the seed of the Christian calendar, arose from the eschatological expectations of the early Church at about the same time as the early succession lists. Thirdly, it has been shown that the mere undated lists of names have their closest analogy in the succession list of the Jewish High Priests, and in particular of the post-exilic High Priests. In this respect it has been shown first that such a list had been compiled in the pre-Christian times. It has also been shown that it arose out of special eschatological considerations, based upon Daniel 9: 24 ff. Also, that the Christian Fathers took a special interest in that list, because they were concerned with that prophecy of Daniel's regarding the seventy weeks before the coming of the Messiah,

just as much as were the Jewish historians. Moreover, in
A.D. 234, Hippolytus included a succession list of post-exilic
High Priests in his Chronicle together with the Jewish
theory that the series of post-exilic High Priests was the
χριστὸς ἡγούμενος. Finally, a curious coincidence of lists
of fifteen names has been stated, and it is surmised that this
coincidence points to the conclusion that the number
fifteen had a special meaning in the lists of Jerusalem and
Rome, and that Hippolytus rejected the list of fifteen plus
six names from the return from Babylon to the time of
Herod, because he objected to this analogy. All these facts
point to one and the same conclusion—namely, that our
inquiries will have to be directed to a Jewish-Christian
source for those ideas which resulted in the compilation of
the early lists of episcopal succession.

# 3

## *The Witness of the Fathers before Irenaeus*

AT the end of the second century there were, as we have
seen, at least four complete lists of the Apostolic succession of bishops: at Jerusalem, Antioch, Alexandria, and
Rome. When Eusebius, at the end of the third century,
used them as the basis for his Canon as well as for his
*Ecclesiastical History*, he regarded them as evidence for the
universal acceptance of the doctrine of the Apostolic succession; but it has been shown that they came into being
only in the course of the second century. The possibility
exists therefore that these four great sees had pushed forward
the doctrine of the Church by compiling those lists, and
that other districts did not yet hold the theory of the Apostolic succession. Of these four great lists, the Roman, contained in Irenaeus' third book against all heresies, is of a very
early date. Irenaeus, we know, was not the author of this
list; it was due rather to the efforts of Hegesippus, who had
also compiled an earlier and shorter list of bishops of the
circumcision at Jerusalem, which Eusebius preserved in his
*Ecclesiastical History*, regardless of the fact that he had
included in his Canon the longer and later list of fifteen
names, which is also to be found in his *Ecclesiastical History*.
These two lists compiled by Hegesippus, the Roman list
and the shorter list of only three names of the Jerusalem
bishops of the circumcision, are the earliest succession
lists we possess, and direct our interest in the development
of the Apostolic succession to Jerusalem and Rome. The
list of Antioch which we possess is of a more recent date;
but this Church provides us with a highly developed theory
of the Apostolic succession, the effect of which made itself
felt in the consecration of bishop Palut of Edessa, at the
hands of the Patriarch Sarapion of Antioch, about A.D. 200.[1]
On the other hand, it will be seen that Edessa as well as

[1] F. C. Burkitt, *Early Eastern Christianity* (1904) 35.

# The Witness of the Fathers before Irenaeus

the churches of Asia Minor held different views until the end of the second century. The list of Alexandria is alone in not having the support of the early Fathers, and the development of this Church will therefore be discussed in a separate chapter.

In the first decades of the second century, well before the complete destruction of Jerusalem under Hadrian, there was born the man who became one of the principal agents in the dissemination of the doctrine of the Apostolic succession—Hegesippus. The fact that Hegesippus was a Palestinian, having Aramaic as his native language, is practically undisputed. Eusebius (*H.E.* 4. 22. 8) attests that he was a Jew by birth. He made a journey to Rome, where he arrived under Pope Anicetus. On the journey he communed with very many bishops, as he himself says (*ib.* 4. 22. 1). He was still alive under Pope Eleutherus, in whose reign he wrote his five books of *Hypomnemata*, fragments of which are still extant, mainly in Eusebius' *Ecclesiastical History*. At Rome, so he says, he compiled a list of Roman bishops; and he assures us that "in every city and in every succession things were as the Law, the prophets, and the Lord proclaim" (*ib.* 4. 22. 3). As the earliest succession lists were only just being formed at that time, we may well assume that his enthusiasm led him to establish several of these lists. The way in which he proceeded is illustrated by his reference to the succession at Corinth (*ib.* 4. 22. 2), where, as we know from 1 *Clement*, mon-episcopacy had not yet been established at the end of the first century.

The Church of the circumcision was plainly the background of Hegesippus. Too much attention has been paid in modern times to the Jewish Christian sects as being the main—or even the only—continuation of the Church of the circumcision.[1] Hegesippus witnesses to the fact that the Church at Jerusalem, which until the martyrdom of bishop Symeon, the successor of St. James, had been a "virgin Church", was disrupted on this occasion, because "The-

[1] The very essence of this one-sided approach may be found in that excellent handbook, R. Knopf, *Nachapostol. Zeitalter* (1905) 1–30. The appreciation of the Church at Jerusalem by Canon B. H. Streeter, *Primitive Church* 38 ff., also omits the whole problem, although on p. 41 ff. the pseudo-Clementine Homilies are rightly accused of being "party propaganda".

boutis began to destroy the Church on account of the fact
that he had not been made bishop".[1] This is a most valuable
piece of information on a somewhat obscure subject. What
had happened was that after bishop Symeon's death a
man who was not of the house of David, Justus, had been
made bishop of Jerusalem. This deviation from tradition
had, of course, engendered a fair amount of jealousy. It is
obvious that even Hegesippus himself strongly deprecated
this apparent break with an established custom.[2] He not
only gave a highly idealized description of the martyrdom
of St. James (Euseb., *H.E.* 2. 23. 4 ff.), and a similar one of
that of bishop Symeon (*ib.* 3. 32. 2 ff.), but he also held that
the sons of St. Jude after their confession before the Emperor
Domitian "ruled over the Churches, being martyrs and of
the family of the Lord".[3] He did not claim that they were
bishops, but he derived their authority from the fact that
they belonged to the family of Jesus. Among these eulogies
the highest praise was given to St. James, and this idealiza-
tion of St. James by Hegesippus was accompanied by a
sharp attack upon St. Paul. Hegesippus appears, therefore,
in close alliance with the numerous anti-Pauline Jewish
Christian sects.[4] Nevertheless, his orthodoxy was expressly
attested by Eusebius (*H.E.* 4. 8. 1.), and Hegesippus should
therefore be taken as a representative of that part of the
Church of the circumcision which was merged into the
Catholic Church.

It is of great importance that Hegesippus saw in St.
James the true successor of the High Priest, "the only one
who had the right of entering the Holy Place" (Euseb., *H.E.*
2. 23. 6). On the other hand, St. James "took the see of
Jerusalem after the assumption of our Saviour" (*ib.* 3. 5. 2),
in the same way as it is so often said by Eusebius that a

[1] Euseb., *H.E.* 4. 22. 5, cf. the preceding paragraph and *ib.* 3. 32. 7 ff.
[2] Euseb., *H.E.* 3. 35. "Justus being one of the myriads of circumcised
believers", plainly echoes the disdain of Hegesippus.
[3] Euseb., *H.E.* 3. 20. 6; 32. 5; cf. K. Holl, *S.B. Berlin* (1921) 935 ff. The
*evocatus* who brought the sons of St. Jude before the imperial tribunal was an
officer of the imperial police. The title is found on papyri of the second century;
cf. Preisigke-Kiessling, *Woerterb.*, vol. 3 s.v.
[4] Anti-Pauline, Routh, *Rell. Sac.*, 2nd ed., 1. 219, from Photius. Anti-
Pauline sects, the Ebionites, 1f. Euseb., *H.E.* 3. 27. 4, the Severians, *ib.* 4. 29. 7 ff.,
and various others.

certain bishop was the first or second after an Apostle.[1]
These two sayings, therefore, define the way in which
Hegesippus regarded the position of St. James as that of
*vicarius Christi*. This exceptional position of St. James is
further enhanced by the report of Eusebius (*ib*. 3. 11) that
the first appointment of a bishop to be made by the Apostles
for the Church at Jerusalem was that of Symeon when they
assembled, together with the other surviving disciples of
the Lord, at Jerusalem after the death of St. James. This
report should be credited to Hegesippus, because it is needed
for the explanation of an uncertainty in the verbatim
quotation of his *Hypomnemata* (*ib*. 4. 22. 4).[2] This is all the
more likely, because the exaltation of St. James was not too
popular in Gentile Christian circles. (Eusebius himself
offers an ambiguous evidence with regard to the question of
his primacy.) The alleged assembly of the eye-witnesses at
Jerusalem after the death of St. James for the consecration
of Symeon is therefore to be regarded as Jewish Christian
propaganda, intended to exempt St. James from being
relegated to the secondary rank of a mere bishop.[3] Of course,
there exists no historical evidence to prove that St. James
was ever called *episcopus* by his contemporaries; it is characteristic of Hegesippus, however, that he called him by that
title, and yet supported his primacy over the Apostles.
This fact serves as a pointer to the source of that theory of
the Apostolic succession which eventually made Eusebius
place the name of St. James at the head of all the episcopal
succession lists.[4]

The intrinsic probability of a Jewish Christian origin of

---

[1] E.g. Annianus, first bishop of Alexandria after St. Mark, *H.E.* 2. 24; Linus,
first bishop of Rome after St. Peter, *ib*. 3. 4. 8; Ignatius, second bishop of
Antioch after St. Peter, *ib*. 3. 36. 2.

[2] The uncertainty in Hegesippus is found *ib*. 4. 22. 4, where we are left to
guess who the *pantes* were who elected Symeon.

[3] K. Holl, *S.B. Berlin ph. hist.* (1921) 935 ff., has drawn attention to this
fact. His evidence, however, is insufficient. Decisive is the change from Hegesippus' saying that St. James received the bishopric of Jerusalem "*amongst* the
Apostles" (μετά), Euseb., *H.E.* 2. 23. 4, to Eusebius' own "*by* the Apostles"
(πρός), *ib*. 2. 23. 1.

[4] In this respect it is worth mentioning that Hegesippus found an immediate
application of certain O.T. prophecies to St. James "the Just", especially one
of Is. 3. 10 (LXX), "let us bind [Hegesippus writes: put away] the just man,
for he is a hindrance to us", Euseb., *H.E.* 2. 23. 15, cf. also *ib*. 2. 23. 7.

the early episcopal succession lists is therefore reinforced by the fact that the author of the two earliest of these lists that have survived was a Palestinian of Jewish descent, who felt a very special loyalty to the Church at Jerusalem and a rather strong antipathy to St. Paul. This was by no means a purely academic attitude, for the doctrine of the Apostolic succession of the bishops was not yet universally accepted, even after the publication of his *Hypomnemata*.

The divergence of views may be illustrated by the comparison of two contemporary documents—namely, official letters of the bishops Narcissus of Jerusalem and Polycrates of Ephesus. The matter under discussion was the date of Easter, and the recipient of both these letters was Pope Victor I of Rome. This matter certainly called for reference to the authorities from which it had received support through the tradition of an unbroken succession of bishops, beginning at the time of the Apostles. This indeed was the force of the argument of bishop Narcissus, who referred to "the Apostolic tradition come down through succession unto us"; but it is surprising that bishop Polycrates did not use this argument, but referred to "the tradition of my relatives, some of whom I have succeeded: for seven of my relatives have been bishops and I am the eighth."[1] This should go a long way towards proving that at the time of Victor I, in the last two decades of the second century, some of the Churches in Asia Minor had not yet a settled theory of the Apostolic succession. The same applied to the Church at Edessa. It is true that the Syriac *Doctrina Addai* mentions a successor who was instituted by this Apostle, but it is more probable that this was added in later times, rather than that Eusebius in the Greek version of the legend should have omitted it twice. It therefore seems wiser not to follow Professor Burkitt, who accepted the succession after Addai as being historical, but to assume that Palut, who was consecrated by bishop Sarapion of Antioch, was the first bishop at Edessa who was within the Apostolic succession.[2]

[1] Euseb., *H.E.* 5. 25 (Narcissus); *ib.* 5. 24. 6 (Polycrates).
[2] Abgar legend, Euseb., *H.E.* 1. 13; 2. 1. 6 ff. F. C. Burkitt, *Early Eastern Christianity* (1904) 33 "that the succession of the bishops of Edessa was broken mainly because of heathen persecution." It is not, indeed, evident either that there had been any succession of bishops, or even that there had been any bishops at all at Edessa before the arrival of Palut.

If at the end of the second century not only the border
districts in Eastern Syria but even so old a Pauline foundation as Ephesus had not yet embraced the doctrine of
Apostolic succession, despite Tertullian's assertion (*Praescr.
Haer.* 36): *si potes in Asiam tendere, habes Ephesum,* surely, an
examination of the origins and the gradual dissemination of
the doctrine is called for.[1] This research will have to consider
negative testimonies, the *argumentum e silentio,* as much as
positive ones. Now, in connexion with Ephesus, the most
important relevant statement is that the Catholic tradition
knows of no line of succession after St. Paul. It is perfectly
true that some other Apostles, even some of the Twelve,
are not credited with having established a line of succession
of bishops any more than did St. Paul. It is also true that
until the days of Cyprian of Carthage Rome regarded St.
Peter and St. Paul as joint founders of her line of succession;
nevertheless, something remains to be explained, if there
is no succession after the Apostle of the Gentiles, particularly
in view of the fact that a definite attempt to establish such
a line of succession had been made in the Pastoral Epistles.
In Eusebius' *Ecclesiastical History* 3. 4. 4 ff., we find a large
catalogue of friends of St. Paul, saying that Timothy became
bishop of Ephesus, Titus bishop of Crete—a rather vague
description, based solely upon the Epistle to Titus—and that
Crescens was sent to Gaul, but the idea of an Apostolic
succession is only introduced when we hear "Linus has
already been mentioned as having been made first bishop of
Rome after St. Peter" (*ib.* 8). Equally noticeable is the
hiatus in the case of Dionysius the Areopagite, for we find
in Eusebius' *Ecclesiastical History* two quotations from
Dionysius of Corinth, saying that he had been made "the
first bishop of Athens", and in both quotations the words
"after St. Paul" are absent.[2]

In order that we may see still more clearly the significance
of this omission, it should be compared with the fact, already
mentioned, that in Eusebius' Canon the first name placed
at the head of all the episcopal lists was that of St. James of

[1] The difference should not go unnoticed, which exists between Tertullian's
somewhat vague reference to Ephesus and the definite statement, *Praescr.
Haer.* 32 *sicut Smyrnaeorum ecclesia Polycarpum ab Joanne collocatum refert.*
[2] Euseb., *H.E.* 3. 4. 10; 4. 23. 3.

Jerusalem. There is an obvious contrast here between the Apostle of the Gentiles on the one hand, and the head of the Church of the circumcision on the other, the first founding numerous Churches, yet at the same time establishing no single line of Apostolic succession, and the other never leaving Jerusalem, and yet heading all the four principal lists of the Apostolic succession of bishops. This contrast is enhanced when we turn to the question: What was the theory of the missionary work of the Apostles in the second century? At the time of Eusebius the apocryphal Acts of the Apostles had become discredited. They had been taken up by the Manichees to replace the canonical Acts of St. Luke.[1] Eusebius was therefore rather reserved in his attitude towards them. It is nevertheless clear that he knew them and regarded them as historical evidence for the deeds of the Apostles. In his *Ecclesiastical History* 3. 1. 1 ff., he reported the division of the mission field as follows:

> Among the Holy Apostles and disciples of our Saviour, who were scattered over the whole earth, Thomas, as tradition has it, had been allotted Parthia, Andrew Scythia, John Asia, where also he eventually died at Ephesus. 2. Peter appears to have preached to the Jews who lived dispersed over Pontus, Galatia, Bithynia, Cappadocia, and Asia; and finally, having come to Rome, he was crucified head downwards, being granted to suffer in that fashion. 3. What need is there to speak of Paul who delivered the joyful message of Christ from Jerusalem to Illyricum and was afterwards martyred at Rome under Nero? All this is said verbatim by Origen, in the third book of his commentary on Genesis.

A. Harnack[2] in discussing this passage hesitated to attribute the whole of it to Origen, because he had overlooked the fact that the five names mentioned, those of St. Thomas, St. Andrew, St. John, St. Peter, and St. Paul, are the five of whom we still possess early, i.e. second-century, Acts. Once this answer is given to what Harnack calls the riddle of the passage, i.e. why only those five names are mentioned, it appears that the whole of it is one single quotation—not two, as Harnack suggests—giving a most valuable indication that no stigma was attached to the use

---

[1] M. R. James, *Apocryphal New Testament* (1926) 228.
[2] *Mission*, 4th ed., 1. 109 ff.

of these Acts at the time of Origen. It is true that Tertullian[1]
took exception to the Acts of Paul and Thecla, which formed
part of the early Acts of St. Paul, but it is doubtful whether
his report, tainted as it is by Montanist resentment, is
sufficient evidence to discredit their orthodoxy. It is also
true that the Acts of Thomas and John are not free from
Gnostic influence, but even they should not be treated as
irreconcilably unorthodox.[2] All these apocryphal Acts were
written, so it seems, in Asia Minor, and in their original
form not one of them made any mention of an Apostolic
succession. Whatever the experiences and adventures of the
Apostles—and they were very varied indeed, including
as they do the baptism of a lion and other wild animals by
St. Paul—they contain no mention of any consecration of
bishops.[3]

Here, in Asia Minor, there existed another idea, that of
the Apostolic succession of Christian prophets after St.
Philip, who was represented as one of the Twelve, although
the person meant was clearly the father of the prophetic
daughters, the so-called evangelist and deacon, the member
of the Seven. The traces of this idea are almost obliterated,
but reference is made to it in an anonymous pamphlet
against the Montanists, excerpts of which are preserved in the
*Ecclesiastical History* of Eusebius. This is what it says:

> The Montanists will be unable to point to any of the prophets of
> the Old Covenant, or of the New, as having prophesied like that,
> neither Agabus nor Judas nor Silas, nor the daughters of Philip, nor
> Ammia of Philadelphia, nor Quadratus; neither will they boast of
> any others, who in no way agree with them. 4. . . . and if as they
> say the women with Montanus had succeeded to the prophetic
> *charisma* after Quadratus and Ammia of Philadelphia, let them produce
> those who are now among them, who are in succession after Montanus
> and those women (5. 17. 3).

[1] Tert., *Bapt.* 17.
[2] I regret very much that I have to differ as to the date as well as the orthodoxy of these Acts from such an authority as M. R. James, *op. cit.* XIX ff.
However, the quotation of Eusebius from Origen leaves little choice on either
of the two questions. All these five apocryphal Acts are second-century and
"at a pinch" orthodox.
[3] Only the late additions to *Acta Joh.* 14; 111, Bonnet 2. 1, 159 ff.; 210,
have the consecrations of Polycarp and Verus. How late the latter is may be
seen from the spurious Epistle of Titus, M. R. James, *op. cit.* 226b, which still
mentions "Verus the deacon".

It then continues, pointing out that between the death of
Maximilla, their last surviving prophetess, and the publication of the pamphlet, i.e. during an interval of fourteen
years, no prophet had arisen among the Montanists, although
they claimed that the prophetic *charisma* should never fail
until the final *parousia*.[1]

Among the prophets mentioned here attention should be
drawn to Quadratus, because he seems to have had information about the foundation of the early Churches in
Asia Minor, which sheds light upon the reasons why the
Apostolic succession of bishops was not universally accepted
by the Churches there. This Quadratus, who is probably
identical with the author of the earliest Christian apology,
but who should be distinguished from the bishop of Athens
of the same name, was said to have been a pupil of St.
Philip's. It is reasonably certain that he had first-hand
information about the early missionaries in Asia Minor, as
he lived in the last years of the first and the beginning of
the second century.[2] Now, this man claimed that the great
majority of Christian churches had been founded by the
generation which had followed the Apostles. "Who, being
the competent pupils of these great men, built the churches
upon the foundations laid in every place by the Apostles"
(Euseb., *H.E.* 3. 37. 1). This second generation produced
the evangelists (*ib.* 2) and they appointed the local pastors,
whereas they themselves wandered from place to place
(*ib.* 3) and their names were lost to posterity (*ib.* 4). This
report is supported by the description of the Apostles and
prophets in the *Didache* (11. 3 ff.) and by the reference to
the "notable men", *ellogimoi andres*, in 1 *Clement* 44. 3, who
had established the local ministries—of whom more will be
said in the course of this chapter.

Local tradition in Asia Minor, therefore, had no notion
of an Apostolic succession of the local ministry. The early

[1] The reference to the *apostolos* who had promised this, Euseb., *H.E.* 5. 17. 4,
is obscure. Was Montanus known as the Apostle? For it is obvious that this
statement is in contradiction to 1 Cor. 13: 8, *Justin. Dial.* 53. 3, quoted below,
seems to refer to Deut. 18: 15 ff., when he discusses the same promise as having
been made to the Jews.

[2] The *Apology* of Quadratus was submitted to Hadrian (A.D. 117–38),
Euseb., *H.E.* 4. 3. 1.

missionaries, the pupils of the Apostles, had not been stationary, and the authority which they claimed was the authority of the Spirit, by which they worked miracles and established local pastors. It was from Antioch that a very different idea of the Apostolic ministry was propagated.[1]

It is to be regretted that, of the various apocryphal Acts of the Apostles, that group which is known as the pseudo-Clementine literature has been excluded from the publications of M. R. James as well as of Hennecke. The *Homilies* have still to be read in Lagarde's somewhat antiquated, unattractive, and very rare edition. Frankenberg's edition of the Syriac Recognitions too, despite his elaborate Greek version of the original, makes it hard to form a mental picture of the whole, co-equal with James's excellent English versions of the other comparable Acts.[2] Nevertheless, the careful reader will discover that the Coptic *Acts of St. Paul* with their dialogue between St. Peter and St. Paul (James, p. 286 ff.) lend support to the assumption that the pseudo-Clementines had an anti-Pauline bias. For, if there is evidence for a discussion going on in the second century between the two great provinces of Asia Minor and Syria in favour of either St. Paul or St. Peter, we are delivered from the unpleasant feeling that the partisanship for a Jewish-Christian, "Petrine", point of view in the pseudo-Clementines came awkwardly *post festum*. For the middle of the second century is the earliest, and at the same time most probable, date of origin for these writings.[3]

The fact that the early apocryphal Acts on the one hand and the pseudo-Clementines on the other were actively opposed to each other is important, because the pseudo-

---

[1] Antioch has been proved to be the place of origin of the pseudo-Clementines by E. Schwartz, *Z.N.W.* 31 (1932), 178.

[2] *Pseudo-Clement. Homilies*, ed. P. de Lagarde (Leipzig, 1865); *Recognitions*, ed. W. Frankenberg (*T.U.* 48. 3, 1936).

[3] On the date of the original of the Ps. Clementines I follow H. Waitz, *Ps. Klementinen* (*T.U.* 25. 4, 1904), who on pp. 40 ff. gives a useful catalogue of Origen's quotations from the original, showing that it dates well back in the middle of the second century. Regarding the anti-Paulinism of Ps. Clement, there is at least one undeniable tilt at St. Paul in *Hom.* 17. 19 Lag. 167. 33 ff.: "if having seen and been taught by Him for an hour, you became an Apostle, you should preach His words, love His Apostles and not fight against His follower. For you are opposing me, the solid rock, the foundation of the Church." These are words of St. Peter addressed to Simon Magus.

Clementines have the Apostolic succession very much at heart. In pseudo-Clement St. Peter is represented as having instituted a bishop at every change of scene. The description of how this was done is of a particular interest, because the pseudo-Clementines take us right back to the time when the earliest succession lists were being compiled. It is, therefore, important to notice that in each case St. Peter is said to have consecrated only one bishop to each see. It may confidently be held that this was due to the teaching of Ignatius of Antioch, who, by his letters and his martyrdom, had firmly established mon-episcopacy. Next comes the observation that the candidates for each bishopric were chosen from the group of presbyters who had accompanied St. Peter since his departure from Jerusalem. It is true this group received one new recruit in the person of Clement, but only under miraculous circumstances. Otherwise all these bishops were members of the Church at Jerusalem. This observation brings together two testimonies which historically are fairly far apart, the succession of presbyters in the Pastoral Epistles and the repeated mention of a succession of presbyters made by Irenaeus, which will be discussed in a later chapter. The third characteristic is the exalted position accorded to St. James. Not only in the correspondence of St. James which forms the introduction to the *Homilies*, but also in the *Recognitions* (4. 35), St. James is granted the primacy as "the Lord and bishop of the Church", or as "bishop of bishops". We remember that St. James was put at the head of all the lists of episcopal succession in the Canon of Eusebius, and we find in the pseudo-Clementines the elements for the explanation of this fact. The original of the pseudo-Clementines was in agreement with the close connexion between the episcopal succession lists and the succession list of the Jewish High Priests. In this respect the two titles given to St. James are of special interest, for it can be proved that they were both fashioned after titles of Christ. The first is closely related to 1 Peter 2: 25: "the shepherd and bishop of your souls", because "Lord" and "shepherd" are both royal titles and easily interchangeable; and the other is closely akin to the title of *pastor pastorum* and *sacerdos sacerdotum*, which were

both used by Hippolytus for the description of Christ.[1] On
the other hand, it is equally significant that Tertullian used
*episcopus episcoporum*, however sarcastically, for a description
of the Roman Pope Callistus.[2] It seems that the position
of St. James was exalted above the other Apostles, because
he was seen as Christ's successor in His priestly ministry.
This was emphasized by that comparison between Christ and
Moses which was popular in the circles from which the
pseudo-Clementines took their origin. We find in *Homilies*
3. 70 (Lag. 55. 19 ff.) the command to respect "the throne
of Christ" as much as "the cathedra of Moses", and it is
obvious that the analogy between Moses and Christ would
give rise to a similar one between Aaron "the brother of
Moses" and St. James "the brother of Christ".[3]

It has to be remembered that the throne was also a
prerogative of the Twelve (Matt. 19: 28), a group of which
St. James was not a member, and it is here that cracks
appear in the construction of the pseudo-Clementines. It is
in the third Homily, 60 ff., where Zacchaeus is consecrated
bishop that these incongruities occur. For in this context
Zacchaeus is enthroned in St. Peter's chair (*ib.* 63 Lag. 53.
25 ff.); but St. Peter asks in his prayer that "he who will be
enthroned upon the chair of Christ may faithfully rule His
Church" (*ib.* 60 Lag. 52. 29 ff.). Therefore, although the
title of *archon*, which Zacchaeus refuses to accept, but which
St. Peter eventually fixes upon him, is clearly taken from
the Jewish Synagogue,[4] the person of St. James is left
completely out of consideration. It appears that the author
of the pseudo-Clementine Homilies subsequently became
aware of the incongruity, for he wrote the introduction of
his work in the form of an official report to St. James. In

---

[1] Hippol., *Benedict. Jacobi* (*T.U.* 38, 1911) 12, 14 ff.; *Comm. Dan.* 4. 31. 2.

[2] Tert., *Pud.*, 1. 6. H. Leclercq, in Cabrol, *Dict.*, 5. 1. 948, referring to
Sidon. Apollin., *Ep.* 6. 1 (5th cent.), calling his friend, bishop Lupus, *episcopus
episcoporum*, seems to be off the right track.

[3] So Euseb., *H.E.* 7. 19, where it is claimed that St. James' chair was still
extant at Jerusalem. Cf. Gal. 1: 19, "James, the brother of the Lord."

[4] Archon, *Hom.* 3. 64; 67 Lag. 53, 31 ff.; 54. 24 ff. The word, although common in Hellenistic Greek, is nevertheless plainly Jewish in this context; cf.
E. Schuerer, *Gesch. d. Jued. Volkes*, 3rd. ed., 3, 47 ff. *Vicarius Christi:* who disobeys the bishop, disobeys Christ, *Hom.* 3. 66; *Ep. Jac.* 2; 17 Lag. 54, 17; 6,
35 ff.; 11, 30 ff.

this report the institution of Clement to the see of Rome was related to St. James as the head of the whole Church. The origin of this discrepancy between St. Peter and St. James should once more be traced back in the first instance to the church at Antioch, that alleged foundation of St. Peter's, where bishop Ignatius had held that each bishop was in his own church the vicar of Christ.[1]

The pseudo-Clementines illustrate the mind of the early Catholic Church in the Roman province of Syria. It is clear that the influences of early Jewish-Christian thought played here a very important part. The prominence of St. James as well as the use of the title of *archon* for the bishop makes it clear; and it is also evident that the idea of the Apostolic succession belongs to the same body of opinion. The geographical limitations of the range of the Antiochene theory are emphasized when we turn to parallel traditions. We possess in the *Vercelli Acts* a Latin version of what originally constituted a chapter of the early *Acts of St. Peter*.[2] They contain the story of the conflict between St. Peter and Simon Magus at Rome. The earlier stages of this conflict form the background of the pseudo-Clementine literature. The two documents are therefore closely related, and it is all the more significant that the *Vercelli Acts* are devoid of any allusion to the Apostolic succession. On the other hand, there is the story of Clement in Syriac, which A. Mingana has published and which he regards as being of early third-century origin. It contains the story of the dispersal of the family of Clement and of its subsequent reunion through the exertions of St. Peter, but the Apostolic succession is once more absent.[3] In the case of the *Vercelli Acts* it is most likely that they—in their original form—constituted one of the sources from which the pseudo-Clementines were compiled. The Syriac story, on the other hand, was an adaptation made from the original of the pseudo-Clementines. In both instances these parallel traditions illustrate the fact that the Church of Antioch, and probably of the entire Roman province of Syria, differed from its neighbouring

---

[1] *Church Quarterly Review* (1945) 117 ff.
[2] M. R. James, *op. cit.* 300; 304 ff.
[3] A. Mingana, *Rylands Bull.* (1917).

districts by the prominence which it accorded to the Apostolic succession. It seems, moreover, that at the time when the pseudo-Clementines were written, the Church of Antioch was only just coming to the fore among the partisans of the Apostolic succession. Reasons have been given in an earlier publication,[1] why Ignatius of Antioch, from his proposition that the bishop was the *vicarius Christi*, would not easily arrive at a theory of Apostolic succession; and as a matter of fact he never proclaimed such a theory. It has also been stated in the second chapter of this book that the Antiochene list of bishops was more recent than that of Rome or the shorter list of Jerusalem. The list of Antioch—unhistorically—put St. Peter at its head in conformity, so it seems, with the pseudo-Clementines, but in contradiction to the canonical Acts of the Apostles, which are silent on this point. All this goes to show that at Antioch the idea of an Apostolic succession was an importation from elsewhere.

Rome produced the earliest witness of the theory which has survived. The pseudo-Clementines have taken us to the middle of the second century. The gap between the Apostolic period and that during which the succession lists were compiled, has thus been narrowed to about eighty years, the time which elapsed between the sack of Jerusalem by Titus and the reign of Antoninus Pius, under whom the pseudo-Clementines seem to have been written by Jewish Christians who had escaped from the second destruction of Jerusalem under Hadrian. The only sources available for these eighty years are the early Apologists and the Apostolic Fathers. There is no evidence for the idea of an Apostolic succession in the writings of the Apologists. Perhaps this is no great surprise, because it is obvious that in the apologetic writings there was little scope for an exposition of the constitutional details of the Church. A fact worth stating is that Justin Martyr in his Dialogue with Trypho made special mention of the succession of the Jewish High Priests and prophets:

> For you say that, although Herod hailed from Ascalon, there was yet among your people a High Priest; and there was for you, according to the Law of Moses, a man offering the sacrifices and observing the

[1] *Church Quarterly Review* (1945) 119 ff.

commands of the Law, and as there were prophets, one succeeding
the other until John [the Baptist], just as in the days when your people
were led to Babylon, after the country had been conquered and the
sacred vessels taken, so also there should never fail to be a prophet,
who would be *kyrios* and *hegoumenos* and *archon* of your nation. (*Dial.*
53. 3.)

It is easy to find in this passage a reference to the χριστὸς
ἡγούμενος, but it is also clear that the succession principally
envisaged was that of the prophets. As Justin Martyr is
generally and justly regarded as a representative of the
Roman point of view in the middle of the second century,
his remark shows that the Church at Rome still treated the
question as to which was the authoritative succession with
an open mind.[1] For just as the *Chronicle* of Hippolytus contained a list of Jewish prophets—and another of prophetesses
—along with its list of Jewish High Priests, so also did
Justin, ninety years earlier, refer to both these successions,
except that he stressed the succession of the prophets in
preference to the priestly succession.[2]

This comprehensive approach to the question of succession
on the part of the early Roman theologians should be borne
in mind when we examine the witness of the Apostolic
Fathers. Just as it sheds light upon the wavering of Pope
Victor I in his attitude towards Montanism, so it also
explains the very remarkable difference between the two
earliest Roman Fathers with regard to the Apostolic
succession. For just as among the apocryphal Acts, so also
among the Apostolic Fathers, there is a marked discrepancy
in that respect. Only one Father, 1 *Clement*, mentions the
doctrine. All the others show no notion of it. Not only is the
Didache silent, but Ignatius also, despite his fervent zeal

[1] Justin's remark merits a comparison with Herm. *Vis.*, 3. 1. 8, where the
woman representing the Church overrules his excuse that the seat of honour
belongs to the presbyters. K. Holl, *Ges. Aufs.* (1928) 2. 69 n. 1, underestimates
the polemical character of this passage.

[2] It is of course true that, the scene of the dialogue being set at Ephesus,
the preferential treatment of the prophetic succession may have been a com-
pliment to the *genius loci*. However, the *Dialogue* was written after the "first"
*Apology* (addressed to Antoninus Pius and M. Aurelius) many years after the
discussion had taken place (A.D. 132–5, during the war of Bar Kochba), and
probably at Rome. If the prophetic succession had been of no account at
Rome, Justin would not have mentioned it.

for mon-episcopacy. Silent is Polycarp; while still more significant is the silence of Hermas, the other Roman among these early Fathers. 1 *Clement*, on the other hand, not only hints at the doctrine, in an imperfect and tentative way, but uses it clearly and competently, as a well-established tenet of the Christian faith. This fact defeats the argument of Dom Gregory Dix, that the Apostolic Fathers, being somewhat simple folk, were unable to express the doctrine which they held all the same.[1] For if, as will be seen, 1 *Clement* held this belief not as his own but as a traditional one, and if 1 *Clement* was as popular as Canon Streeter has rightly stressed, especially at Antioch,[2] the silence of his more recent companions has to be explained in a different way.

1 *Clement* differs from the pseudo-Clementines in that it omits all references to St. James. The important passages are to be found in chapters 42 and 44. There, in 42. 2, he states that "as Christ is of God, so the Apostles are of Christ", and therefore need no scrutiny of their credentials by their fellow Apostles. He further maintains (*ib.* 4) that the Apostles "constituted their first-fruits, having tested them, as bishops and deacons for the faithful to come". This he proves by an incorrect quotation of Isaiah 60: 17 to have been divinely predicted. Continuing, he asserts that the Apostles had established a law—or made a will—concerning the succession to their ministry (*leitourgia*, 44. 2), and says that the successors had been ordained by the Apostles or by other "eminent men" (*ellogimoi andres*, 44. 3).[3] Thus the doctrine of the Apostolic succession was here fully established, and the important question is why it was not even mentioned by the other Apostolic Fathers—and not to what degree this plain evidence is admissible.

---

[1] *Apostolic Ministry* 187. Cf. how a great critic like Eusebius distinguishes between the simplicity of Papias, *H.E.* 3. 39. 13, as compared with the greatness of Ignatius of Antioch (*ib.* 3. 36. 2 ff.).

[2] *Primitive Church* (1929) 152 ff.

[3] In 1 *Clem.* 44. 2, I read *epinomis* for *epinome*, which has the meaning of by-law, *lex* in the ancient Latin version, and may also be explained by *epinomos*, the heir, which is frequent in inscriptions. There is no justification for the "bold" translation of *ellogimoi* by Dom G. Dix on p. 256 n. 3. It is neither supported by the further use of the word in 1 *Clement*, nor by other Hellenistic sources, as e.g. Philo, *Vita Mosis* 1. 246; Philostr., *Vitae Sophist.* 1. 9. 1. ; 2. 11. 1.

The reason why 1 *Clement* incorporated the doctrine of
the Apostolic succession in his admonition of the Corinthian
Christians was because of its dependence upon Jewish-
Christian convictions. The falsification of Isaiah 60: 17 in
1 *Clement* 44. 4 has been justly compared with similar
practices in Philo.[1] Moreover, the idea of an Apostolic
succession in 1 *Clement* forms part of a repeated attempt to
prove that the ministry of the Church was the continuation
of that of the priests and Levites in Israel. In particular
1 *Clement* 43 is given over to the description of how Moses
founded the ministry in Israel, and how this is the pattern
of Christ's creation of the new ministry of the Church. In
this respect 1 *Clement* is closely related to Hebrews 3, where
Christ is represented as the *apostolos* of God. The Jewish
character of this description of Christ is enhanced by a
comparison with the contemporary *Assumptio Mosis* 18,
where Moses is called the *magnus nuntius* of God.[2] Consequently 1 *Clement* appears as being closely related to
Jewish-Christian ideas and, in the question of the Apostolic
succession at any rate, far removed from Hermas, which
was its somewhat more recent Roman companion among
the Apostolic Fathers. This divergence will not surprise
anybody who is aware of the fact that the Church at Rome
in the second century was already more comprehensive
than homogeneous.[3]

By this analysis of 1 *Clement* 42 and 44, we are able to
establish a connexion with the Epistle to the Hebrews
which is regarded by many as addressed to Jewish-Christians
at Rome. In this Epistle Christ is represented as the great
High Priest, combining the priesthood and the kingship,
according to "the order of Melchisedec", in much the same

[1] F. Gerke, *Stellung d. 1. Klemens* (*T.U.* 47. 1, 1931), 83; cf. how 1 *Clement*
41. 3, stresses the author-right of the doctrine, A. Harnack, *Kirchenverf.* 53.
[2] Moses, cf. Tert., adv. *Marc.* 4. 24, *tamen enim apostolus Moses, quam apostoli
prophetae*; Euseb., *H E.* 1. 3. 2. Cf. also the derivation of the title of Christ
from Moses in Hippol., *Comm. Dan.* 4. 30. 8; Tert., *Bapt.* 7.—The Jewish-
Christian element in 1 *Clement* is stressed in an almost forgotten article by
L. Lemme, *Jahrb. Deutsche Theologie* 1 (1893), 371 ff., and more recently by
K.Mueller, *Abh. Acad. Berlin phil. hist.* (1922) No. 3, 3 ff.
[3] Cf. Dom G. Dix, Hippolytus, *On the Apostolic Tradition* (1937) XXVII n.,
and in particular the brilliant article by G. La Piana, *Harv. Theol. Rev.* (1925)
201 ff.

way as Aristobulus and Alexander Jannaeus had combined priesthood and kingship. If it be held that the "angels" of the Seven Churches in Revelation were in reality bishops, but that their title was formed analogously to that of the ancient Jewish High Priest,[1] there is thus another line of communication between 1 *Clement* and one of the late writings of the Apostolic period. In any case, the closest analogy to 1 *Clement* 43 is to be found in the comparison between Moses and Christ in Hebrews 3. This comparison was at the same time, so it seems, a real stumbling-block for the Christians who had been Gentiles. There are two very interesting remarks on the Apostleship of Christ, originating from Alexandria, which may illustrate the perplexity of the Gentile Christians. Clement of Alexandria, as quoted by Eusebius, referred to the "blessed presbyter" (i.e. Pantaenus) who had held that as Jesus had been the Apostle to the Hebrews, so St. Paul had been the Apostle of the Gentiles (Rom. 11: 13);[2] and Origen probably had this saying in mind when he proposed his theory of the Apostleship of St. Paul, attempting to reconcile it with the more orthodox temper of the Alexandrian Church of his days, saying:[3]

> From Christ, so St. Paul says, he did receive grace and the Apostolate, as from the Mediator between God and men. . . . "Grace" has to be referred to his patience under suffering, and the Apostolate to the authority of his preaching. For Christ Himself is called an Apostle, i.e. sent by the Father, even claiming to be sent to preach the Gospel to the poor. . . . And as it is said of Him, "having therefore the High Priest and Apostle of our profession, Christ", so He grants to His disciples the dignity of the Apostolate, that they should be made the Apostles of God.

Here we have a modification of the theory quoted from "the blessed presbyter" Pantaenus by Clement without any accusation of heresy. Origen corrected his master by limiting the comparison between Christ and His great Apostle to the one instance of his Apostolate. In this respect, however, he holds that their task was identical, viz. "to preach the Gospel to the poor". Origen made this statement with regard to St. Paul, and not to St. James and the

---

[1] *Church Quarterly Review* (1945) 115 ff.
[2] Eus., *H.E.* 6. 4. 1.
[3] Origen, *Comm. Rom.* 1. 7. Lo. 6, 30 ff.

Twelve. It is therefore closely connected with the views held by the Gentile Christians, and must not be used as evidence for ideas which are intrinsically Jewish, even if a superficial analogy to the Jewish Apostles should be discernible. The Western Church, inspired by the Roman doctrine of 1 *Clement* which eventually won the day, used much stronger language. Tertullian exclaimed, *tam enim Moyses apostolus quam Apostoli prophetae*, "Moses is just as much an Apostle, as the Apostles are prophets."[1] These different voices echo the discussion in which, on the one hand, the sacerdotal character of the Apostolic ministry was derived from Christ, the High Priest and Apostle, and on the other, the discussion in which an unsuccessful attempt was made to create a succession after St. Paul. They also lend colour to the fact that Clement of Rome was chosen as the hero of the pseudo-Clementines, the Christian from the Gentiles who had accepted the claims of the Jewish-Christians. The strength of this appeal may be measured by the fact that Tertullian, omitting the names of Linus and Anencletus, made Clement the immediate successor of St. Peter at Rome.[2] This fact will also be discussed more fully in a later chapter.

So far the result is that there were conflicting views with regard to the doctrine of the Apostolic succession as far back as the last decades of the first century, when the author of 1 *Clement* lived. They may even have left their marks upon the later Apostolic documents, for instance upon the Epistle to the Hebrews and the Apocalypse. The doctrine conquered Antioch in the middle of the second century. At Rome it was admitted even earlier, but with a characteristic modification. The person of St. James was left out, and this rift was not even closed by the pseudo-Clementines. Only the letter to St. James at the beginning

[1] *Adv. Marc.* 4. 24, cf. Euseb., *H.E.* 1. 3. 2, explaining how Moses made known by prophecy the name of Christ, when he called the High Priest, the type of the Lord, by the name of Christ.

[2] The process is exactly the same as in the *Doctrina Addai*, where it is said that Palut was consecrated by Sarapion of Antioch, who in his turn had been consecrated by Zephyrinus of Rome, "the man chosen by St. Peter to follow him after his twenty-five years' tenure at Rome." To W. Bauer, *Rechtglaeubigkeit und Ketzerei* (1934) 22, all this is "gibberish", but we may recognize the pattern on which myths of this kind were formed in the early Church.

of the pseudo-Clementine Homilies paid a belated tribute to the first monarchical head of the Church at Jerusalem by the head of the Church at Rome. Asia Minor, on the other hand, had a different doctrine of a prophetic succession, and Roman theologians like Justin Martyr were still at liberty to proclaim it in the middle of the second century. At Alexandria, too, theories of a very different kind seem to have been current, countering the anti-Paulinism which was an inherent element in the doctrine of the Apostolic succession. The fate of the doctrine was therefore in the balance, and the scales were tipped in favour of its acceptance first by the Montanist crisis, which stayed the hand of the Church in Asia Minor, and secondly by the exertions of that very remarkable man Hegesippus, the author of the Roman succession list.

The combined witness of Hegesippus and the pseudo-Clementines, together with Eusebius' Canon putting St. James first among all the bishops, is evidence for the origin of the doctrine of the Apostolic succession. Hegesippus knew 1 *Clement*,[1] but this knowledge did not affect his claim for the supremacy of St. James. The pseudo-Clementines took their name from Clement of Rome, but preferred the fabrication of the letters of St. James to St. Peter and of Clement to St. James to the abandonment of this claim. This energy, displayed at a time when "the bishops of the circumcision" were already a thing of the past, is proof of the unshakable conviction among the members of the Church at Jerusalem that an unbroken succession after the Jewish High Priests was essential for the New Israel, the Church. The comparison with the Mahometan Caliphate, so popular among recent authors for the description of the position of St. James at Jerusalem,[2] overlooks the fact that the priesthood was at the root of the Apostolic succession. In this respect St. James was superior to the other Apostles, for it was not before Irenaeus that it was claimed that "priests are all the Apostles of the Lord, who inherit neither estates nor houses here, but always serve the altar and the Lord." Moreover, this statement, for which there

---

[1] This is expressly stated by Euseb., *H.E.* 3. 16.
[2] Cf. B. H. Streeter, *Primitive Church*, 40.

is no Biblical foundation, can only be referred to the heavenly Church.[1] St. James, on the other hand, in the midst of his presbyters, as described for instance in the *Codex D*-version of Acts 21: 18, was indeed the model of an early Christian bishop, as much as the image of the Jewish High Priest. Consequently, as all the available evidence regarding the origins of the doctrine of the Apostolic succession points in the direction of the Church at Jerusalem, we venture to draw the conclusion that the source of this doctrine is to be found in the circle round St. James and his successors of the circumcision. The doctrine owed its impetus to the necessity of continuing the sacerdotal ministry of the Old Israel within the New Israel, the Church. It was a bequest on the part of the Church of the circumcision to the Catholic Church, making it evident that Rabbinic Jewry, because it had cut loose from the official succession of High Priests, had become a schismatic sect, whereas the Church, continuing it, was the true inheritor of the gifts of God bestowed upon the Old Israel. For this reason the succession at Jerusalem started from the beginning as a monarchical one, a true succession of bishops in fact, if not in name. Among the Gentiles, on the other hand, it was first a succession of presbyters, sometimes called bishops, as in Acts 20: 28. The laying on of hands cannot be proved as having formed part of the consecration rite in the earliest times, although the evidence from the Pastoral Epistles as well as from the *Apostolic Tradition* of Hippolytus makes it probable that the rite was continued during the period between the times of origin of these two testimonies. It was, however, the enthronement which seems to have been regarded by the pseudo-Clementines as the constitutive act. This view is supported by the claim that the original chair of St. James had been preserved at Jerusalem; and this is also the reason why Rome made a similar claim in respect of the chair of St. Peter, however much the curiosity of pious pilgrims may have contributed to the making of such claims.[2]

[1] Iren., *Adv. Haer.* 4. 17 H. 2, 167 ff. A similar statement by Origen, *Hom. Lev.* 7. 1. *Werke* 6. 373, 8 ff., belongs nevertheless to a new development, in the course of which the positions of Apostle and bishop were more and more harmonized.

[2] Cf. B. H. Streeter, *op. cit.* 42 ff.

# 4

## The Prophetic and other extra-regular Ministries

THE recognition of the Apostolic succession of bishops presupposes that episcopacy as such was a recognized constitutional principle within the Church. That was the case in the early Catholic Church, but it was so only as the result of a process of unification which had been going on during the first two centuries. At the end of this period the threefold ministry of bishop, priest, and deacon was more or less accepted everywhere, and the Apostolic succession of bishops was well on its way to becoming the hall-mark of orthodoxy, as opposed to heretical and especially Gnostic sects. However, there is a fairly general absence of clarity with regard to the way in which this result was achieved, and a widespread suspicion that the Apostolic succession was the chief instrument by which priest-craft with its low cunning eradicated that "charismatic ministry" which by right should govern the Church. For this reason it seems appropriate to inquire into the way by which earlier ministries, which now appear as "extra-regular", were superseded by episcopacy. The arguments in favour of the existence of a so-called "charismatic ministry" will also be examined.

There are three types of these "extra-regular ministries", the transitional, the emergency ministries, and the ministries of martyrs, gnostics, and virgins, which were based upon their several vocations. Of all these ministries only one was systematically suppressed, that of the prophets; all the others were fitted somehow into the framework of the Church hierarchy. It will also become evident that in the whole process of assimilation the idea of the Apostolic succession was not invoked.

To begin with the transitional ministries in the early Church, these were of different kinds. There were some

83

which were of necessity transitional—for instance, that of the evangelist, or missionary, which had the intention of establishing a Church capable of producing an indigenous ministry. These will be discussed later on. There was, on the other hand, the famous triad of apostle, prophet, and teacher in 1 Corinthians 12: 28, which disappeared within the first two and a half centuries, although it is probable that St. Paul regarded these ministries, rather than those of bishops, priests, and deacons, as being of the essence of the Church. Among this triad the prophetic ministry and its fate deserves our closest attention. The disappearance of the Apostolate is understandable. For the visitations of His disciples by the risen Lord ceased—with the one exception of that at Damascus—after His ascension, and there were therefore no new creations of genuine Apostles. It is, however, just this analogy of the termination of the Apostolate which makes it hard to believe that only material reasons put an end to the prophetic ministry. Somehow it seems insufficient to say with Harnack[1] that "the Montanist movement brought the apex and the end of early Christian prophecy", without giving a reason. An inquiry into the special task of the prophetic ministry within the early Church will show in what way the Montanist crisis led to the conclusion of the prophetic ministry under the New Covenant.

A valuable collection of the sources, pagan as well as Biblical, containing the word *prophetes* has been contributed by E. Fascher,[2] who, on the whole, has shown a commendable restraint with regard to the conclusions which he has drawn from the collected material. His sources show that the early Christian prophecy had come to an end by the close of the second century. After this time there were no more prophets to be found within the Catholic Church. Unfortunately, Fascher has accepted as a reason for this the very common view that by that time the manifestations of the Holy Spirit ceased to be forthcoming. Although this view would provide us with the required analogy to the ascension of Christ and the resultant termination of His visitations to His Apostles, it has to be said that this is just

---

[1] *Mission*, 4th ed., 1. 363, cf. *Kirchenverf.* 96.
[2] E. Fascher, *Prophetes* (1927).

not true.[1] It cannot be held with any kind of conviction
that the miraculous manifestations of the Divine Spirit have
ever been wanting within Christ's Church, and a generation
like ours would be particularly ungrateful if it failed to
recognize the prophetic quality in men like Archbishop
William Temple, Karl Barth, and Albert Schweitzer.
There seems to be no reason either to believe that experiences
which had been so frequent at the time of the Apostles and
which showed themselves as strongly under the pressure of
persecution as they did among the desert Fathers (witness
the various Acts of the Martyrs and the whole literature of
*Apophthegmata*) should have been withheld for a period just
long enough to complete the final termination of the prophetic ministry.[2] All these theories have been possible only
because no one has realized that it was not prophecy itself
but the prophetic ministry which vanished. On the whole,
Church historians have been well satisfied with the use of
the word "prophet" without inquiring into its meaning,
and even Fascher's careful collections of sources have not
caused any radical change.

The New Testament prophets had a twofold task. In the
Acts of the Apostles we find them charged with special
messages of the Holy Spirit. Such was the case, when the
prophets at Antioch, Acts 13: 1 ff., disclosed to St. Barnabas
and St. Paul the command of the Spirit to proclaim the
Gospel to the heathen. The same was true with regard to
Agabus, when he gave his warning about the great dearth to
come under the Emperor Claudius, Acts 11: 28, as well as

---

[1] Almost amusing is the assertion made by many, e.g. E. Friedberg, *Kirchen-recht*, 4th ed. (1895), 17 n. 71, but also by Harnack, *Zwoelf Apostel-Lehre* (1884) 123 ff.; 127, and elsewhere, that the Christian prophets had "died out", like the Dodo.—Admirable is the description by C. H. Turner, *Studies in Early Church History* (1912) 13 ff.; 31 ff., of the way in which the "universal" ministry of the prophets was assimilated by the local ministry.

[2] Equally unconvincing is the psychological argument for the termination of the prophetic ministry proposed by many who believe that the loss of con-fidence in the prophets, shown by the warnings of the Didache and Hermas Mand. 11, created a similar loss of self-confidence in the prophets, and finally became the cause of their complete disappearance. It seems to me that the Christians of that time inclined rather to credulity than to the opposite, and that the warnings mentioned, together with the satires of Celsus and Lucian, should be understood as evidence for this credulity. They are, at any rate, much older, Matt. 7 :15; 2 Pet. 2: 1; 1 John 4: 1.

the prophecy of the danger threatening St. Paul at Jerusalem, Acts 21: 10. It appears, however, from 1 Corinthians 14: 29 ff., and especially from Revelation 10: 11, with its allusion to Jeremiah 1: 10, that the prophets were also allotted a general task of proclaiming the Christian message for all times.

When we attempt to define the character of the prophetic ministry within the early Church, we have to start from two points. The first is to be found in the excerpt from an anti-Montanist writer (Euseb., *H.E.* 5. 17. 3) which makes it clear how the Montanists claimed that there had been a succession of prophets and prophetesses within the Church. Additional support is given to this first point by the two lists of Old Testament prophets and prophetesses respectively which were to be found in the Chronicle of Hippolytus, as well as by the fact that in the Chronicle of Africanus the list of the Jewish kings was accompanied by entries indicating the succession of their contemporary prophets.[1] The second point is that according to the teaching of the Church the quality of prophet was an indelible character, which gave its holder a special status within the Church. It was not just an accidental happening by which the Holy Spirit used any one Christian for His pronouncements. This point is most clearly brought out in Hippolytus' *De Antichristo* 2, "for all those who have been endowed with the prophetic spirit and have been duly honoured by the Logos Himself, and have been joined together like members, always hold the Logos in their inner man, like a *plektron*, which moves them to pronounce the will of God." The same conclusion may be drawn from two polemical remarks of pseudo-Clement, and it is also supported by Jewish as well as by pagan sources.[2]

[1] On the anti-Montanist cf. C. H. Turner, *op. cit.* 16 ff. Chronicle of Hippolytus, cf. E. Caspar, *Bischofsliste* 94. Africanus, *ib.* 102. Prophetesses were not only frequent in heretical circles, like that Jezebel of Rev. 2. 20, the Helena of Simon Magus who, according to Ps. Clem., *Hom.* 13. 15 Lag. 138, 22 ff., had been a pupil of St. John the Baptist, or the Philumene of Apelles, cf. Euseb., *H.E.* 5. 13. 2; Tert., *Praescr. Haer.* 6 fin; *De Carne* 24; *Adv. Marc.* 3. 11, but also among the Catholics, cf. A. Harnack, *Mission*, 4th ed., 1. 363 n. 3.

[2] Hippol., *Antichr.* 2 *Werke* 1. 2, 4, 19 ff. Ps. Clem., *Hom.* 2. 10; 3. 13 Lag. 24. 15 ff.; 39. 29 ff. In *Kirchenverf.*, 19, Harnack has stated the *character indelebilis* of the early prophetic ministry, but has omitted to give any evidence. An interesting parallel to it is the application of the same principle to Holy Baptism n *Didask. Lat.* 6. 21. 3. Jewish, cf. how the expected prophet was to supersede even the appointed High Priest, according to 1 Macc. 14: 41. Pagan, cf. R. Reitzenstein, *Poimandres* (1904) 219 ff.

These two observations make it clear that the early Church regarded the prophetic ministry as a real ministry which it expected to continue.[1] The prophet held the second rank after the Apostle within the primitive Church, according to 1 Corinthians 12: 28, and his ministry was a universal ministry in a way similar to that of the Apostles. The universality of the prophetic ministry appears just as clearly as its indelible character in Hippolytus' *De Antichristo* 2, where it is said that it was not the prophet's task to preach for the present moment only, but to proclaim the eternal truth for all times. In this respect Christian doctrine found itself once more in complete agreement with Jewish opinion, and in particular with Philo.[2] This is important because it explains the fact that the early Christians apparently found no difference between the prophets of the Old Covenant and the New. In Justin's *Dialogue with Trypho* this view lay behind the argument that the Jews had had no more prophets since the days of Christ, whereas the prophetic spirit had been much in evidence within the Church.[3] It may, therefore, be said with confidence that the New Testament prophets appeared to those early generations of Christians as continuing the ministry as well as the teaching of the Old Testament prophets. Their universality was not so much a geographical as a temporal one. They were charged with proclaiming the truth of Christ's Gospel for all times. In accordance with this, Hermas, who may be regarded as the prototype of the early Christian prophet, produced his apocalypse, which was destined to serve the whole Church; and in Justin's *Dialogue with Trypho* reference was repeatedly made to the continuation of the Old Testament prophecy by the prophets of the early Church.[4]

This analogy was stressed by the early Fathers, when they put forward their idea of a succession of the prophets. Their starting-point was, as we have seen, the succession of Joshua after Moses, accepted by the Christians as well as by the

[1] Prophets belonging to the hierarchy, C. H. Turner, *op. cit.* 13.
[2] Philo, *Vita Mosis* 1. 277, cf. E. Fascher, *op. cit.* 155.
[3] Justin, *Dial.* 51.
[4] Cf. especially *Dial.* 82, "for among us are the prophetic gifts (*charismata*), by reason of which you must understand that, what was previously the prerogative of your nation, has been transferred to us".

Jews. The awkward part, however, was the gap between the
last of the Old Testament prophets, Zechariah or Malachi,
on the one hand, and John the Baptist on the other. It has
been seen how in the *Chronicle* of Hippolytus the early
Christian prophets were merely added to an earlier Jewish
list. Justin Martyr, however, chose a different way:

> Trypho: "It seems inconclusive to me that you say, that the prophetic
> spirit from God which was in Elijah, was also in John."
> I replied: "Do you not think, that the same took place in Joshua,
> the son of Nun, who succeeded Moses in the leadership of the nation,
> when Moses was bidden to lay his hands upon Joshua by the promise
> of God, I will transfer upon him part of the spirit which is in you?"
> Trypho: "Certainly."
> "If therefore", I replied, "when Moses was still among the living,
> part of the spirit which was in him, was transferred upon Joshua by
> God, the spirit was also able to go from Elijah to John." (*Dial.*, 49.)

We may add that this argument excluded the necessity for
any outward and visible sign of prophetic succession, but
it insisted all the more strongly upon the identity of the
prophetic spirit under the Old and New Covenant.[1]
Allegorical descriptions, like that drawn from Hippolytus'
*De Antichristo* 2, that the Holy Spirit acted like the *plektron*
upon the lyre, served to enhance this kind of succession,
which joined the links of the chain through the identity of
the spirit. Whether or not this succession in the spirit was
accompanied by a formal ordination of prophets is still a
matter for conjecture. There is no direct evidence for it, but
it may be claimed that the analogy of Moses and Joshua
inspired the ordination of the Jewish Rabbis through the
laying on of hands, which is practised to this day. Moreover,
the characteristic addition to the warning of James 3: 1,
"be not many teachers, my brethren", by which pseudo-
Clement, *Virg.* 1. 11. 4, cautioned his readers, "neither be
you all prophets", may also point in the same direction, if
it be assumed that the ministry of teacher was conferred
upon a person by ordination. On the other hand, Montanus
and his two prophetesses claimed to be the successors of
Quadratus and Ammia without any ordination, and indeed
did not ordain any successors. If, therefore, an ordination or

[1] A formal consecration of prophets took place, nevertheless, among the
*Marcosii*, Iren., *Adv. Haer.* 1. 13. 3, cf. R. Reitzenstein, *Poimandres*, 220 ff.

consecration of Christian prophets was practised at all, it was certainly not compulsory.[1]

The fact that the Old Testament prophets were the model for the prophetic ministry within the early Catholic Church may be used to explain certain constitutional features which appear with regard to the position of a prophet within a local Church. The overriding authority which was granted to him was the same in Did. 13. 3, as in 1 Maccabees 14: 41, where even the High Priest Simon Maccabaeus was elected to his office only "until God should raise up a true prophet". As the Didache (11. 11) expressly insisted upon the identity of the prophets under the Old and New Covenant, this analogy with one of its most characteristic commands ought not to go unnoticed. It supports Harnack's suggestion that, as in Acts 15: 22 and 32, so also in 1 Clement and in Hermas *Vis.*, 2. 2. 6; 3. 9. 7, the title of *hegoumenoi* or *prohegoumenoi*, leaders, may have been a circumscription for prophets.[2] This title of leader lends a great deal of colour to the complaint made by Hermas that the false prophets demanded for themselves the *protocathedria*, the first place of honour. Such a demand on the part of a true prophet was reasonable because the analogy to the Old Testament prophet meant nothing less than that the new prophets were also supposed to be infallible in their pronouncements. Their infallibility was stated *expressis verbis* by pseudo-Clement, and was presupposed even in an author as late as Tertullian, when he apostrophized Marcion in the following manner: *si propheta es praenuntia aliquid, si apostolus es praedica publice, si apostolicus senti cum apostolis.*[3]

It seems a *petitio principii* to assume that this exalted position of the early Christian prophets was forcibly brought to the level of the local ministry. It is much more likely that there was a gradual assimilation of the two in the course of the evolution of local Church government. There were two

---

[1] A case point in may be the ordination of Timothy "by prophecy", 1 Tim. 1: 18; 4: 14; cf. E. Fascher, *Prophetes* 171. Cf. also *ib.* 118 ff., on the Old Testament origin of early Christian prophecy.

[2] Harnack, *Zwoelf Apostel-Lehre* 94 n. 8; cf. on the relation between High Priest and Apostle *ib.* 128.

[3] Hermas, *Mand.* 11. 12, cf. Harnack, *op. cit.* 129. Infallibility, Ps. Clem., *Hom.* 2. 11 Lag. 24. 20 ff. Marcion, Tert., *De Carne* 2.

ways in which the prophetic ministry tended to combine with the local ministries. On the one hand, the prophets took up responsibilities in the local Churches. The Didache shows that the prophets were concerned with the distribution of alms among the poor, and Th. Zahn has reasonably suggested that this may have been a general usage.[1] On the other hand, Hermas in his eleventh Mandate castigated false prophets for the seclusion in which they prophesied for money (11. 11), answering private inquiries about the future (11. 2), and rarely, if ever, entered "the assembly of just men", i.e. the ordinary Christian congregation (11. 13),[2] but gathered their own little crowd in some remote corner (*ib.*). The true prophet, he says, was an ascetic who gave no private oracles, but prophesied only in "the congregation of just men" (11. 9). This combination of prophecy with the ordinary worship had been instituted already at Corinth by St. Paul (1 Cor. 14: 24),[3] who probably intended to bring about in due course the absorption of the prophetic *charisma* by the local ministries. Subsequently we find in Asia Minor a marked tendency to combine the prophetic ministry with that of the bishops. Other parts of the Church may have followed suit. It is at any rate unwise to quote Hermas as protesting against this tendency because he said (*Mand.* 11. 12) that the false prophets, who always sat upon a *cathedra*, claimed the *protocathedria*, whilst the true prophets only occupied the pews. Neither[4] can his remark (*Vis.* 3. 1. 8) be used as proof that at his time the established ministry had already gained a strong ascendancy over the prophetic ministry: "Lady, let the presbyters sit down first." Probably both these passages were intended only to show up the boastful contempt of the false prophets for the ordinary Christians and to stress the humility of the true prophet. In Asia Minor, on the other hand, there was not only Melito of Sardes who combined the episcopate with the prophetic *charisma*,[5] but also Polycarp of Smyrna, who is described in his *Martyrium* (16. 2) as an "apostolic and prophetic man".

---

[1] *Did.* 15. 3 ff. Th. Zahn, *Forsch. z. N. T. Kanon* 3 (1884), 301 ff., cf. *ib.* 302 n. 1, on the analogy of St. Stephen.

[2] Cf. M. Dibelius, *Hdb. z. N. T. Erg. Bd.* (1923) 541.

[3] R. Reitzenstein, *Mysterien Relig.*, 3rd ed. (1927), 239.

[4] This remark is directed against K. Holl, *Ges. Aufs.* 2, 69 ff.

[5] Hieron., *Viri Illustr.* 24.

The tendency to combine the prophetic ministry with the
episcopate signified a progressive decomposition of the
ancient, universal ministry of prophet, which added greatly
to the authority of the prophet-bishops. Polycarp's ministry,
for instance, penetrated far beyond the borders of the city
of Smyrna. His teaching was universal even in a geographical
sense, as appeared on his visit to Rome, when he stilled the
first dissension about the date of Easter; and it is certain
that men like Irenaeus accepted it also as truly prophetic,
particularly because he was in succession after St. John,
"The Apostle and prophet", as he is called in Hippolytus'
*De Antichristo*,[1] the same St. John whom Church tradition
saw in the role of bishop of Ephesus.

In this way a slow amalgamation of the prophetic ministry
with the episcopate was inaugurated, which might well have
ended with the creation of a dogma of infallibility, similar
to that of the Vatican Council, although the crucial question
of the false prophets had already entered as a disturbing
factor. For the false prophets demanded the same prerog-
atives as the true, and there arose the disquieting task of
discerning the spirits. In this respect the advice given in the
*Didache* 11. 8 is of great importance. It holds that it was the
main quality of the true prophet that he showed forth the
*tropoi*, manners, of Christ. This, we believe, not only presupposed that he showed forth personal humility, which was
so strongly insisted upon by Hermas, but also evidence of a
specific spiritual power.[2] This conclusion is made inevitable
by the example of the Old Testament prophets. The same
example, moreover, points to the very difficult problem
which was involved in the discerning of the spirits, i.e. that
their prophecies were proclaimed not only by word of mouth
but also in written form. It has to be realized that the early
Christian Apocalypses, and in particular that of St. John, were

[1] Hippol., *Antichr.* 50 *Werke* 1. 2, 33, 14; cf. C. H. Turner, *op. cit.* 15, on the
prophetic character of the Revelation of St. John.

[2] *Tropoi*, quite insufficient are the remarks of Harnack, *Zwoelf Apostel-
Lehre* 124, who refers only to Herm., *Mand.* 11, and thinks of no more than an
inoffensive behaviour, to which cf. Christ's own warning of false prophets in
sheep's clothing, Matt. 7: 15. It should be remembered that the LXX use
*tropos* in Num. 18: 7; Dan. 1: 14, as a translation of Hebrew *dabar*, word, and
that Symmachus employs it as a translation for *mishpat*, judgment, in Eccles.
8: 6.

the first Christian writings which were regarded as having an authority similar to that of the Old Testament. The prophetic ministry, therefore, claimed that it continued the divine revelation, and for this reason the false prophets were particularly dangerous. It was therefore agreed that, as *Didache* 11. 2 says, any prophetic instruction which was not intended to teach the Lord should be rejected. This rule concerning the discernment of the spirits is found accompanying the whole evolution of the early Church, from St. Paul saying (Gal. 1: 8): "though we or an angel from heaven preach any other gospel unto you, than we have preached, let him be accursed", to 2 John 9 ff. "whosoever . . abideth not in the doctrine of Christ, has not God; . . . if there come any unto you and bring not this doctrine, receive him not."

It was in connexion with this particular difficulty of the discerning of the spirits that a situation arose which caused the forcible termination of the prophetic ministry in the Montanist crisis of the second half of the second century. The tremendous impression made by the sudden outburst of the prophetic spirit in Asia Minor at that time is brilliantly illumined by C. H. Turner's hypothesis that the remarks about the Christian prophets in the *True Word* of Celsus as well as in Lucian's description of the career of Peregrinus as a Christian were both consciously modelled on the figure of Montanus. However, this is no more than an hypothesis, and perhaps not even a convincing one.[1] Far more important are the observations made by Turner with regard to the many signs indicating that at that time the confessors claimed to possess the special status of the crowned martyrs and threatened to abandon the respect to the established Apostolic ministry. The crowned martyrs had for long been seen in close proximity to the prophets, and even treated as their superiors. It is probable that the Saints in Revelation 18: 20, who are mentioned before the Apostles and prophets, have to be understood as martyrs; and it is certain that Hermas gave to the martyrs the precedence over himself, the prophet. Hippolytus placed martyrs and prophets side by side as "the servants of the Lord, prophets and martyrs", and Hegesippus and Tertullian said that the martyrs were

[1] C. H. Turner, *Studies* 17 ff.; 23 n. 1.

"kinsmen of the Lord", or that "Christ is in the martyr",
two ideas which are similar to the saying mentioned before,
that the prophet had the Logos within him. Turner was
therefore quite right when he maintained that the opposition
of the confessors and the Montanist movement were closely
connected with each other.[1]

In the *Acts of Perpetua and Felicitas*, which are of Montanist
origin, we see the result of the joining of forces by the martyrs
and the Montanists. These martyrs claimed that during
their imprisonment they were granted personal revelations
through visions and similar direct communications with the
Deity, and under this stress the continued recognition of
the prophetic ministry by the Church constituted an ever-
increasing menace. Personal reasons made it extremely
difficult to give an unbiased verdict on these experiences.[2]
The task set before the prophetic ministry under the New
Covenant had been accomplished by the production of the
Revelation of St. John. After that the Christians found
themselves faced with an ever-increasing number of written
prophecies, like those of Barcabbas and Barcoph, which
Agrippa Castor mentioned as the sacred books of Basilides;[3]
and in each case reasons had to be shown why these revelations were not to be regarded as orthodox. The principle
applied almost succeeded in promoting that somewhat
pedestrian Shepherd of Hermas to canonicity, because of
its impeccable orthodoxy.[4] Now Montanus and his two
prophetesses had arisen after a period in which not many
prophets had established themselves in Asia Minor. We
are informed—and that by an adversary—that their pronouncements were not in conflict with Catholic orthodoxy,

---

[1] On Rev. 18: 20, cf. E. Lohmeyer, *Offenbarung* (1926), 149: Hermas, *Vis.*,
3. 1. 9; cf. K. Holl, *Ges. Aufs.* 2, 69. Hippol., *Comm. Dan.* 4. 14. 3, *Werke*, 1. 1,
222, 9 sq. Hegesippus in Euseb., *H.E.* 3. 20. 6; Tert., *Pudic.* 22. Martyrs and
Montanists, Turner, p. 24 n.

[2] K. Holl, *op. cit.* 70 ff., wrongly neglects the Montanist character of the
*Acts of Perpetua*; his assertion, p. 74 ff., that the recognition of the prophetic gift
of the martyrs was only possible when there were no more genuine prophets,
is wrong.

[3] Euseb., *H.E.* 4. 7. 7.

[4] The Montanist crisis caused the final rejection of Hermas' claim to canonicity; cf. M. Dibelius, *Handb. Erg. Bd.* (1923) 419, with reference to Harnack,
*Gesch. Altchr. Lit.* 1, 51 ff.; cf. also B. H. Streeter, *op. cit.* 208 ff.

and, on the other hand, that they were put into writing; further, we learn from Tertullian that they were treated as authoritative.[1] Moreover, these new prophets claimed to continue the succession of the Catholic prophets since the days of the Apostles. St. Philip and his daughters, Quadratus, and the already half-forgotten Ammia were claimed by Montanus and his prophetesses as their predecessors, even though they appear to the modern historian as a very different type of prophet. It was obviously a matter of principle whether or not such additions to the Apostolic canon should be tolerated.

Harnack[2] has accused the Catholics of having used new and unfair arguments in their conflict with Montanus; but their demand to examine whether the prophetesses were truly inspired resulted rather from the very understandable desire to avoid, as long as was humanly possible, any decision upon such an important matter. However, when this escape had been made impracticable by the unflinching refusal of the Montanists to agree to any such examination, the Church, led by its bishops, came to a decision with a vigour which can still be judged from the degree of heresy into which the extremists on the other side were thrown. The main issue was whether or not prophetic books were eligible for the canon of New Testament writings. The Church decided to apply the test of Apostolicity to all the books of the New Testament; but the extremists, the so-called *Alogoi*,[3] refused altogether to recognize the authority of St. John, because of his Revelation. They thus put themselves beyond the pale of Catholic orthodoxy. In any case the result was that the canon was closed to all those apocalypses which, however orthodox they may have been, did not stand the test of Apostolicity. This decision put an end to the prophetic ministry within the Catholic Church. In the West, however, it was made possible only by the assistance rendered by the

---

[1] Orthodoxy of Montanus, Hippol. *Philos.* 10. 25 *Werke* 3, 282, 15 ff. His prophecies put into writing, E. Fascher, *op. cit.* 221. Their authority; cf. how Tert., *Resurr. Carn.* 11, quotes a saying of the prophetess Priscilla as pronounced by the *paracletus per prophetidem.*

[2] Harnack, *Zwoelf Apostel-Lehre* 124 n. 38; 126.

[3] Iren., *Adv. Haer.* 3. 11. 9; Euseb., *H.E.* 7. 25. 1 ff., cf. N. Bonwetsch, *Gesch. d. Montanismus* 23–25.

confessor Praxeas, that is, by the application of the principle of *divide et impera*. As a result of these tactics the famous definition of the Church by Hippolytus mentions the martyrs —together with all those other orders, which were characterized by Tertullian as fallible—as essential members of the body of Christ, but omits the prophets. The reason for this discrimination was none other than the belief in the infallibility of the prophets, which the Church was no longer prepared to admit.[1]

In comparison with the prophetic ministry, the other extra-regular ministries are much less important. The existence of other transitional ministries resulted from the fact that it took the Church almost two centuries thoroughly to assimilate the three Apostolic bequests upon which it is founded—the Creed, the canon of Holy Scriptures, and the ministry. The same process of evolution may still be observed in the case of foreign missions, in the period which precedes the foundation of an autonomous Church and the production of a translation of the Bible and the liturgy in the vernacular. Roman canon law rightly makes special provision for the mission field, and reference to this rule may be of assistance for our understanding of developments within the primitive Church. When the history of the Apostolic ministry is scrutinized from the missionary point of view, it is no longer a surprise that it should have started earlier at Antioch, for instance, than at Edessa, or at Rome than at Carthage. An important, though somewhat secular, consideration in all those cases in which the appointment of a bishop was contemplated was the fact that the bishop was not allowed to follow a profession. He had to be maintained by his flock. It may be assumed that this demand was an important factor in any such development as that described

---

[1] Definition of the Church, Hippol., *Comm. Dan.* 1. 17. 8 *Werke* 1. 1, 28 ff. Tertullian on fallibility, *Praescr. Haer.* 3; cf. N. Bonwetsch, *op. cit.* 18: "when Montanism recognised a canon, it really cut its own life arteries, and therefore appeared in a modified form in Tertullian". K. Holl, *op. cit.* 2. 84 ff., gives an interesting analysis of the differences between the *Acts of Perpetua*—and to a lesser degree the *Martyrium of Polycarp*—which acknowledged a prophetic quality in the imprisoned martyrs, and the later Acts which failed to do so. His explanations, however, are purely psychological: the jealousy of the bishops and the decline in the literary quality of the later *Acts*, and are therefore unconvincing.

by Origen,[1] where the last and crowning act of the foundation of a local Church is said to be the institution of its first missionary as its first bishop. In the meantime, however, the Word had to be preached, baptisms had to be administered, the Holy Eucharist had to be celebrated. These duties were to be performed, so the *Didache* (15. 1) informs us, by prophets or teachers holding a universal ministry. The local bishops and deacons were substituted in their stead, where persons holding a universal ministry were not available. Those local Churches had had for their founders the early travelling missionaries, apostles, prophets, and evangelists, whose aim had been the conversion of all the heathen, the *ellogimoi andres* of 1 *Clement* 44. 3, the second generation of Christian preachers mentioned by Quadratus, the prophet.[2] They had not been appointed by any local congregations or, for that matter, by any local bishops, because these congregations and bishops were only brought into existence through their ministrations.[3] In these cases the ministry existed prior to the Church, and although it had not yet been regularized, exercised its authority at the very moment when the formation of a local Church began. Its authority, unless the missionary had been sent out by another Church, was a purely spiritual one, founded upon the vocation of the missionary by the Holy Spirit, but it had also only a temporary, transitional authority.[4]

The emergency ministry is different, although comparable. Here another modern precedent may be referred to as an explanation. In Hitler's extermination camp at Theresien-

---

[1] Origen, *Hom. Num.* 11. 4 *Werke* 7. 84. 24 ff., "consider . . . how in some town where as yet there are no Christians, someone arrives, and begins to teach, works, instructs, leads to the faith, and finally becomes the ruler [*princeps*, Greek: *archon*] and bishop of his pupils."

[2] Euseb., *H.E.* 3. 37. 3: "they laid the foundations of the faith in foreign parts and nothing more. Subsequently they appointed others as pastors and entrusted them with the cure of the newly won. They themselves, however, went to other countries and tribes by the grace and help of God", etc.

[3] This, by the way, shows the fallacy of any "congregational" theory of the Church.

[4] That was still the case with Pantaenus, the founder of the catechetical school at Alexandria, when he went on his mission to India, Euseb., *H.E.* 5. 17. 2: "for there were at that time still numerous evangelists of the Word, employing enthusiastic zeal in imitating the Apostles in spreading and exalting the Divine Word."

stadt, Christians of Jewish descent formed two Churches, the one Roman Catholic, the other Lutheran. Both were without ordained ministers. The Roman congregation accordingly refrained from holding any regular services which demanded the presence of an ordained priest, whereas the self-appointed leader of the Lutherans administered the Sacraments—in accordance with article 67 of Luther's *Smalcaldic Articles* of 1536–38—although he had not even the necessary elements, but was compelled to use tea instead of wine.[1] This modern instance, which deserves a very careful examination on the part of a trained canonist, may serve as an illustration of cases like those mentioned by Tertullian,[2] when lay people under the cover of darkness held services for the faithful few, who were determined to resist the pressure of State persecution. It will also help to explain how it was that a Catholic presbyter felt no compunction in embodying the legend of the self-baptism of Thecla in his Acts of St. Paul.[3] In cases in which there was a real emergency such ministrations were admitted even by a rigorist like Tertullian, who expressly stated that in the normal way only the heretics would admit laymen to the administration of the sacred mysteries.[4]

Finally, the third type of extra-regular ministries, and the one most heatedly discussed, was that of people claiming a special authority on account of their visionary or comparable religious experiences. It has to be realized that the Apostles did not belong to this category, being men who had received their commission to preach the Gospel by the risen Lord Himself. Whether or not the prophets and teachers of 1 Corinthians 12: 28 and Acts 13: 1 ff. are to be numbered with them is a moot question. It is certain that even from the earliest days of the Church attempts at regulating these ministries were made. Nevertheless, it has to be said that the prophets at least were in close proximity to this group,

---

[1] A. Goldschmidt, *Geschichte der Evangelischen Gemeinde Theresienstadt* (Tuebingen, 1947).

[2] Tertullian, *De Fuga* 14.

[3] Thecla, *Acta Pauli et Theclae* 34, cf. 40 Lipsius, 1, 260 ff.; cf. Tert., *Bapt.* 17 fin.

[4] Tert., *Praescr. Haer.* 41. It is improbable that Tertullian's turning Montanist accounts for the difference from *De Fuga* 14.

the chief representatives of which were the confessors who
had been in chains, the virgins, and the Catholic gnostics.
In each of these cases two questions have to be asked, one
regarding the special qualifications which were demanded,
the other regarding the extent of ministerial functions performed. With regard to the first question, it has to be said
that outward material facts were not the chief criterion.
In each of the three cases mentioned spiritual qualifications
were at stake. This is evident in the case of the gnostics,
where no such outward qualifications were available. It is
equally true in the case of the virgins, for it has been shown
by H. Koch[1] that in the early times no special vows were
made and no order of virgins was recognized by the Church.
Even in the case of the confessors, where the material qualification was strongest, the spiritual was the most important.[2]
These ministries are therefore to be regarded as spiritual
ministries. The second question cannot be answered with
any similar certainty. For instance, when Hippolytus (*Ap.
Trad.* 4) granted the presbyterate to the confessors, it may
have been no more than a special provision necessitated by
the Montanist crisis, granting to the confessors the much-
coveted seat amongst the ordinary clergy. Hippolytus
certainly made no mention of either the preaching of the
Word or the administration of the Sacraments by the confessors. Similarly we may ask, but we cannot decide, whether
Clement of Alexandria when claiming that the Catholic
gnostics were the model for the entire ministry of the Church
—bishops, priests, and deacons—wished to imply that they
also held a ministerial position within the earthly Church.[3]
We can say only that on the one hand the analogy of the
prophets in the *Didache* makes such a conclusion possible,
whereas on the other the fact that the virgins—in contrast to
the widows—were not considered as belonging to the clergy
points in the opposite direction. A definite statement denying ministerial status to the gnostics, which originates from
Origen, will be discussed in a later chapter. It is of importance

[1] H. Koch, *Virgines Christi* (*T.U.* 31. 2, 1907) 65 ff.; cf. *Didasc. Lat.* 3. 8. 3. fin.
[2] R. Sohm, *Kirchenrecht* 1 (1892), 39 n. 5; K. Holl, *Ges. Aufs.* 2, 70.
[3] K. Mueller-v. Campenhausen, *Kirchengesch.*, 3rd ed., 1. 1, 289.

here because it sets a limit to the time during which questions concerning their ministerial functions may be asked.

In all these cases no systematic suppression can be proved. The ministry of the confessors found its natural end at the time of the Decian persecution, when their numbers increased to such an extent that it was no longer practicable to admit them to the presbyterate. The denial of the existence of infallible prophets and the ensuing suppression of the prophetic ministry paved the way for the rejection of the claim of the confessors for preferential treatment.The cutting nature of the remarks in the correspondence of Cyprian of Carthage regarding the indulgences granted by the martyrs to the *lapsi*, although responsible for the schism of Felicissimus, nevertheless represented the conviction of the majority of Catholic Christians. A special status within the hierarchy of the Church was found for the virgins, and the Catholic gnostics served as a model for the later Christian Saints, at least in so far as the written biographies of these Saints are concerned.[1] It appears that neither with regard to their origin nor yet with regard to their destiny is it at all convincing to combine these various ministries under the title of "charismatic ministry". In so far as they involved regular services, they were either transitional or emergency ministries, and were therefore not of the essence of the Church; and in so far as they were part of normal Church life, it cannot be proved that their holders ever performed normal ministerial functions.

It is also doubtful whether the modern term of "charismatic" is at all applicable. It is true that the prophetic ministry was dependent upon a special *charisma*, gift, of the Holy Spirit. Hermas (*Mand.* 11. 9) personified it as "the angel of the Divine Spirit", whereas Montanus, and the author of pseudo-Justin's *Cohortation*, 8, spoke of the Spirit as the *plektron*. Athenagoras[2] called Moses and the prophets the "flutes of God" upon whom the divine *Pneuma* was play-

---

[1] Cyprian, cf. *Church Quarterly Review* (1941–42) 186 ff. T. W. Manson has suggested to me that the privilege of forgiving sins may have been granted to the confessors because it belonged to the presbyters.

[2] J. Geffcken, *Zwei Griech. Apologeten* (1907) 179 ff.

ing, and this idea had its analogy in other early Christian as well as in Jewish and Neo-Pythagorean writings.[1] *Charisma* in this sense had the meaning of distinction and vocation, and it was never so used for any ordinary martyr. On the contrary, it was a special distinction for the martyr Alexander of Lyons that in the letter which his Church wrote on the great persecution in A.D. 177 he was marked out as having an "Apostolic *charisma*". Neither the martyr-bishop Pothinus nor any of his martyr presbyters or deacons were granted this distinction. The close connexion between the word *charisma* and the qualities described as Apostolic and prophetic is also evident from the fact that Ignatius used it in his letters to the Church of Smyrna as well as to its bishop Polycarp, that "Apostolic and prophetic man", but did not claim it for himself.[2] Neither is there any evidence for a special *charisma* of virgins and gnostics.

The evidence from the early Fathers is therefore somewhat discouraging for the supporters of the theory of the "charismatic ministry". There cannot be any doubt that it is an illusion to believe that it ever existed as something comparable to the institutional ministry. This illusion is

[1] Early Christian, *Odes of Solomon* 6. 1 ff.; Ps. Hippol., *De Christo et Antichristo* 2 Lag. 2. Jewish; Philo, *Quis Rer. Div.* 52/3 M. 510, quoted after Reitzenstein, *Poimandres*, 204 n. 1. Neo-Pythagorean, Diotogenes in *Stob. Flor.* 4. 148. 62 Hense 4. 62, "for the well-ordered city must respond to its king like a lyre"; Euryphamus frg. 1 Mullach 1. 15b, "for man's life is like a well-tuned and altogether perfect lyre".

[2] Alexander, Euseb., *H.E.* 5. 1. 49. Ignat., *Smyrn. Intr.;* Polyc. 2. 2. In Ignat., *Eph.* 17. 2, as in *Act. Just.* 15. 2, and 1 *Clem.* 38. 1, *charisma* is used as a synonym for *charis.* Just., *Dial.* 88. 1, shows the same, whilst in 82. 1 the word once more refers to the prophets. Iren., *Adv. Haer.* 2. 32. 4, uses the word for all the benefits which the Church distributes among men. Tert., *Praescr. Haer.* 29, uses it in a similar way, whilst *adv. Marc.* 5. 8, he singles out the special *charisma* of tongues. In his pamphlet against the Valentinians 4 fin., the so-called revelations of the Gnostics are denied the quality of *charisma*, a remark referring to the prophetic *charisma*. Significant is the contrast he made between martyr and prophet *adv. Prax.* 1 *de iactatione martyrii inflatus . . . dilectionem Dei non habens cuius charismata quoque expugnavit.* Hippol., *Philos.* 8. 19. 2, saying that the Montanists praised their prophetesses "above the Apostles and every *charisma*", once more shows the close connexion between the Apostolic and prophetic gifts. Finally, Origen, *Comm. Rom.* 7. 5 Lo. 7, 106 ff., saying that "the Apostle St. Paul had called the many spirits *dona vel gratias* of the Holy Spirit", developed the idea found first in Hermas that the prophetic *charisma* was the angel of God sent to the prophet.

derived largely from the contrast between the two ideas of the general priesthood of all believers, on the one hand, and the succession of the bishops and the priests to the priesthood of the Old Covenant on the other. The question whether or not these two ideas are irreconcilably opposed may be left open. Our task is to find out whether the Apostles ever intended to authorize a "charismatic ministry". This can be done only by an examination of the meaning of the word *charisma* in the New Testament. There is no doubt that "charismatic" is a modern invention; *charisma*, on the other hand, is found fifteen times in the New Testament, mainly in St. Paul's Epistles, with the one exception of 1 Peter 4: 10. The word has a wide range, combining all the manifold gifts of grace granted by God in the redemption of man through Jesus Christ. Viewed from the angle of the complexity of the term, it may be held that its choice for describing the combination of all the extra-regular ministries has not really served the purpose of elucidation. In three texts *charisma* may be understood as meaning the appointment to a ministry within the Church: in 2 Corinthians 1: 11, where it probably means St. Paul's Apostolate, and in 1 Timothy 4: 14 and 2 Timothy 1: 6, where it denotes Timothy's ordination. Both these cases belong to the sphere of the institutional and not to that of any "charismatic" ministry.

No other passage can be mentioned where *charisma* possesses the connotation of ministry; but the adherents of the theory of the "charismatic ministry" have used the meaning which can be derived from these three passages for their interpretation of 1 Corinthians 12: 4 ff. and Romans 12: 6 ff. undisturbed by the far more numerous cases in which *charisma* has nothing whatsoever to do with any ministry. In that way they have reached the conclusion that the ministries within the primitive Church were among the *charismata* of the Spirit enumerated in these texts. This conclusion can be proved wrong without more ado in the case of 1 Corinthians 12, as the various ministries in 1 Corinthians 12: 28 ff. are co-ordinated with—not subordinated to—the special *charismata* which are found in vv. 28 and 31. Therefore, unless we allow for an exceptional lack of clarity, it is impossible to believe that the general conception of *charisma* was used for all the ministries mentioned in these verses, and at the same time for one of the minor ministries which appear in that context.

In Romans 12: 6 ff. also, the term of *charismata* does not touch upon the institution of the ministry as such, but upon the effectiveness of the work of the appointed minister. For this reason St. Paul insisted that "as ministers, they shall perform effective service; as teachers, give instruction; as comforters, give comfort; when distributing reliefs, perform their duties honestly; when presiding, be diligent in their administration; when doing welfare work, do it cheerfully." The whole emphasis lies upon the effective performance of the ministerial duties, and not upon the question of the ordination or non-ordination of the ministers. However, this question was not passed over by the New Testament. Very enlightening is a little remark in Acts 14: 26, "from there they sailed back to Antioch, where they had been committed to the grace [*charis*] of God for the work which they had done." The reference is to Acts 13: 1 ff., to the laying on of hands upon St. Barnabas and St. Paul when they had been sent out upon their first missionary journey. There had been a formal dedication ceremony and in it the power of the *charis* of the Divine Spirit had been bestowed upon them enabling the two Apostles to administer the *charismata* of the Divine Word, with all the miraculous works connected with its dissemination. The same thought is expressed more clearly still in 1 Timothy 4: 14; 2 Timothy 1: 6, where the *charisma* itself is nothing less than the gift of the Holy Spirit received by Timothy in and through his ordination. In this way the two expressions *charis* and *charisma* appear to be almost synonymous. In each case it is the grace of God working through human agents. The idea of status, which distinguishes the clergy from the laity, has no place in the meaning of *charisma*. This idea has found its expression in the metaphor of the body and its members which St. Paul employs in 1 Corinthians 12: 14 ff. The "charismatic ministry" appears therefore as a *contradictio in adiecto*, and it is to be hoped that the term will soon disappear from the field of the theological discussion.[1]

The idea of a "charismatic ministry" has been expressed in two ways, either as a purely historical description of something which it is supposed was once in existence;[2] or else as something which—perhaps, because it is believed to have existed—ought to exist. In the first case we are faced with a theory which, although it has little to commend it in the light of the available evidence, nevertheless deserves to be tested by a scrutiny of the sources; in the second we are faced with a theological demand which is heretical. It is certain that the interesting fashion in which this heresy has been presented by its author, Rudolf Sohm, has had the effect of stimulating the search for, and the willingness to believe in, the existence of a "charismatic ministry". It is to be hoped that the exposure of the fallacies of Sohm's demand that there ought to be a "charismatic ministry" may diminish the willingness to admit that such a ministry existed in the primitive Church. The ground would then be cleared for a more exhaustive examination of all the various cases in which it is assumed that the free gift of the Spirit qualified a person for the performance of regular ministerial duties without any formal ordination or consecration.

Rudolf Sohm, who was one of the leading figures in the field of the History of Law in Germany at the end of the last century, published two large volumes entitled *Kirchenrecht* (canon law), dealing mainly with the origin and history of canon law. Although these two volumes were published as parts of a series of books under the title of *Handbooks of Legal Science*, it is fair to say that Sohm's intention was to produce a handbook against canon law, which he regarded as the arch-enemy of Christianity. His

[1] The same result is arrived at from an inspection of 1 Pet. 4: 10, where Dean Selwyn, 1 *Peter* (1947), 218 ff.; cf. 415 ff., has rightly stressed that the advice given refers to everyone, but does not preclude the distinction between the clergy and the laity.

[2] This unguarded use of "charismatic" is most popular among German theologians, especially in H. Lietzmann, *Korinther*, 3rd ed. (1931), 63, commenting on 1 Cor. 12: 27 ff. Harnack too may be charged with inaccuracy rather than heresy, when in *Kirchenverf.* 46 he speaks of "*Charismen welche die Kirche begruendeten*", with reference to 1 Pet. 4: 10. But even Dean Selwyn, *op. cit.*, cannot be entirely exonerated from such a charge.

professed belief was that Christ by His fulfilment of the law of Moses had abolished law and had called the Christians to a life in the Spirit. This, so it seems, is neither more nor less than the well-known demand of all mystics that the only directive energy in the life of Christ's body, the Church, should be derived from that guidance of the Spirit which is granted to the faithful elect. This indeed cannot be regarded as a source of law, although Clement of Alexandria tried to treat it as such, when representing the gnostic as the model to be followed by the institutional ministry of the Church. The impression made by Sohm, therefore, was much more the result of his presentation of this idea, which was new, than of his actual protest which was more or less identical with that which earlier mystics had already voiced against the uniform service offered to God by His Church.

The new method of presentation which Rudolf Sohm employed tried to show that the idea of canon law cannot be found in the New Testament, and that therefore canon law cannot be admitted as an authority within a Church which is exclusively founded upon Holy Scripture. If this was the supreme consequence of the extreme protestant position which Sohm took up, it was on the other hand— so it seems—a confusion of categories, because "canon law" is a formal, not a material, principle, which is to be used as a technical help when interpreting the Bible, and not something to be found in the Bible itself. Moreover, Sohm's whole approach was vitiated by his further claim that the introduction of canon law was a revival of the legalistic spirit of the Old Testament, so apparently it was not alien to Holy Scripture. This spirit, which he says had once been conquered by Christ, had been resurrected by the egotism of those self-seeking clergy who had been inspired by the legalistic and domineering mind of Rome. Anti-Roman as well as anti-Jewish prejudices were blended with the mysticism of Sohm. This complexity of aversions has its parallels too in the temper of numerous mystics of earlier times. In consequence his appeal was made to sentiment rather than to reason. Therefore, unless the reader has been so overpowered by sentiment that he will uncritically accept the correctness of Sohm's conclusions, he will not fail to notice the one-sidedness of his approach, even though his book displays exceptional erudition. The constant juggling which is needed to prove that the numerous rules laid down by St. Paul are not canon law, because they do not conform to Sohm's idea of canon law, is stale and unprofitable. Obviously, those rules show neither the technique nor the range of later canons and decretals; it is also true that Christ has delivered man from the yoke of the law of Moses, and that the relation between the law and the Gospel which He has created is one of the central problems of Christian life and doctrine, but that does not prove that this matter has to be thrashed out in the field of canon law rather than in the field of theology.

This brings us to the real point at issue, the theological foundation of canon law. Sohm, who had found that organized church services were uninspiring, opened up a new line of attack upon the clergy of his time by denying the validity of their orders. He hated 1 *Clement*, by whom a similar attempt had been defeated as early as A.D. 96, by the Apostolic decision of the Church at Rome. The only qualification for the ministry, so he said, was the manifestation of the power of the Spirit in the person of the minister. (He seems to have missed the point as to who the adjudicators should be.) Thus he was at bottom in no way different from the innumerable others who, before and after him, have attacked "organized religion". Through his learning he has given a certain impetus to their attacks. For it is now no longer on their level, but on Sohm's, that an answer to his indictment has to be found.

It should be obvious that the comparison between the authority of the canon law within the New Covenant with that of the Mosaic law under the Old Covenant will immediately reveal the flaws in Sohm's argument. For the canon law, whatever its authority may be, is not "the Law" as opposed to "the Gospel". Therefore it has no claim to unchangeableness, a fact which appears most clearly in the abolition of two decrees of the first and most authoritative of all the councils which have ever been held, the council of the Apostles, prohibiting the consumption of blood and things strangled (Acts 15: 28–29). Even the Roman Church has abandoned these two ordinances, although the authority of canon law cannot be put higher in any Christian community than it is there. Nevertheless, its authority is inferior to that of "the Law and the Gospel". The same consideration renders null and void any ordination or consecration, even though performed with the most meticulous attention to detail, if external conditions make it evident that the prayers offered for the gift of the Holy Spirit were said blasphemously, as for instance in cases of simony, or that they were said under compulsion. For the whole ritual, with the laying on of hands as its climax, is to be regarded only as the "outward and visible sign of an inward and spiritual grace". All this, however, does not diminish the importance of the fact that Christ by His incarnation and by calling men to be His fellow workers has sanctified human law to minister unto His kingdom. For human work can be done satisfactorily only in a society which is organized by means of law. This does not mean that the rules of canon law should lay down privileges to be selfishly enjoyed by the clergy; it means that clergy must be endowed with such authority as is necessary for the administration of their special task. Like so many Protestants, Sohm has been led to the false conclusion that existing abuses may invalidate a sound principle, and that pious contemplation can replace that discipline of which at the moment Christ's army, the Church, is showing too little rather than too much.

# 5

## *Irenaeus and his pupils*[1]

MON-EPISCOPACY was victorious against the competition of the extra-regular ministries because it was firmly based on the Old Testament. Its basis contained two elements. The one was the idea of *vicarius Christi.*[2] As the bishop represented Christ in His sacerdotal ministry, he stood in a similar relationship to the Jewish High Priest. In this sense St. John addressed the leaders of the Seven Churches as angels, because the Jewish High Priest was regarded as the *mal'ak*, the angel of God.[3] The other element is the continuation of the sacerdotal succession under the Old Covenant by the episcopal succession under the New, as expressed by the imitation of the Jewish succession lists of High Priests in the Christian episcopal lists. By the end of the second century the title of High Priest had gained a considerable amount of popularity in the Church. In the West it was used by Tertullian and Hippolytus, and in the East by Origen, and is to be found as well in the Syriac Didascalia. All this was not only acceptable but even popular in the Catholic Church.[4]

Irenaeus, who was not more than twenty-five years younger than Hegesippus, incorporated both these ideas in his doctrine of the episcopacy, but tacitly dropped the primacy of St. James, who is conspicuously absent from his

[1] This chapter was written before the publication of E. Molland's article in *J.E.H.* 1 (1950), 12 ff.

[2] Cf. *Church Quarterly Review* (1945) 113 ff.

[3] Cf. W. Bacher, *Aggada d. Babylon. Amoraeer*, 2nd ed. (1913), 21, saying that Rab (died in A.D. 247) held that Michael, the prince of the angels, offered sacrifice continually at the altar of heaven, and that Philo saw the Logos as the High Priest offering intercession.

[4] Tert., *Bapt.* 17; cf. *Pud.* 1, a testimony which is not less valuable for being ironical. Origen, cf. Hatch-Preuschen, *Gesellschafts-Verf.* (1883) 142 n. 60; Hippol., *Ap. Trad.* 3. 4.; *Didasc. Syr.* 2. 25. 7; 26. 2; 4, which in 2. 25. 8 ff. even refers to the analogy of pagan priests.

work against all heresies. There is no doubt that Rome had at that time a doctrine of the succession of her Popes after St. Peter and St. Paul, which the Roman Church was not prepared to subordinate to the primacy of St. James, especially as his succession had been interrupted by the destruction of Jerusalem under Hadrian; and Irenaeus as we know was strongly attached to the Roman cause. This attitude resulted in a considerable widening of the scope of the Apostolic succession. From now on St. James was, in the West, simply added to his fellow Apostles as one among the many who had been entitled to establish an Apostolic succession. This group was not limited to the Twelve, although they were regarded as its champions, but it had to be safeguarded against inflationary tendencies for reasons which were connected with the whole history of the Church in the second century.

When the Church insisted upon Apostolicity as the decisive qualification for the canon of New Testament writings, and for this reason suppressed the infallible prophetic ministry, it was forced to do so by the gnostic menace. The gnostics claimed secret traditions after the Apostles. Basilides based his heresies upon St. Matthias and Glaucias, secretary to St. Peter;[1] Valentinus referred to Theodas, the pupil of St. Paul, as well as to St. John, and Marcion to St. Paul, and the whole approach of Irenaeus in his work against all heresies is conditioned thereby. The danger of secret traditions was countered by explaining the principles by which the apostolicity of Church traditions was tested. The Apostolic canon was presented as the result of a serious and sincere scrutiny of those traditions which were corroborated by the statements of reliable witnesses. Irenaeus solved this gigantic task by his close combination of the Apostolic tradition and succession. He produced the authoritative definition of the Apostolic succession for the Western Church, employing the episcopal succession for the proof of the genuineness of the Apostolic writings, because it was greatly superior to that capricious, erratic "charismatic" succession of the prophets with all its attendant dangers; and he resisted Montanism for the same

[1] On Basilides cf. G. Krueger, *Handb. d. Kirchen-Gesch.*, 2nd ed. (1923), 84 ff.

reason, although the Lyonese martyrs had previously
entrusted him with their letter to Pope Eleutherus, suggesting
a compromise.[1] The result of his critical approach to the
question may be gauged from the Muratorian canon, which,
far from being merely an index of prohibited books, enumerated the titles of those Christian works for which the Roman
Church was prepared to answer; and this type of index was
continued and improved upon in that Church, until the
decree of Pope Gelasius gave it its final form.[2]

Irenaeus, therefore, had "an axe to grind" when he
insisted upon the Apostolic succession, and his witness is
less valuable for the history of the doctrine before his time
than for its formation in subsequent times. His special
interest in the Apostolic succession was the support which
it gave to the Apostolic Creed and those writings which
had been accepted by the Catholic Church. This support
was either direct or indirect. It was direct if it was a succession of witnesses for the Apostolicity of some or all of the
Apostolic writings and teachings which had been accepted
by the Church; it was indirect when it proved the Apostolic
origin of the Catholic Church which entitled it to those
Apostolic writings and teachings. These two sides of Irenaeus'
doctrine of the Apostolic Church may be called the Apostolic
tradition and succession respectively. Irenaeus himself
realized the two-sidedness of his approach. For he employed
both these terms, and sometimes even combined them more
or less closely, as for instance when he said:

> However, when we challenge the heretics with that tradition which
> is kept by the churches through the succession of the presbyters, they
> take exception from tradition, saying that they are wiser not only
> than the presbyters, but even the Apostles. (*Adv. Haer.* 3. 2. 2. H.
> 2, 7 ff.)

Irenaeus here referred for the "apostolic Tradition"—
the direct support of the Catholic Creed and canon—to the

---

[1] Irenaeus nowhere expressly mentioned Montanism, but it seems certain
that in 3. 11. 12 H. 2. 51 ff., where he denounced the *Alogoi*, he described the
Montanists as *pseudoprophetae* (read: *infelices vere qui pseudoprophetas esse nolunt*,
etc.), and in 4. 52. 3; 53. 1 H. 2. 260 ff., they are again the most likely
adversaries. Epistle to Eleutherus, Euseb., *H.E.* 5. 3. 3; 4. 1.

[2] The most convenient collection of the various indices is E. Preuschen,
*Analecta* (1893), 129 ff. Cf. Souter, *Text and Canon of the N.T.* (1913) 205–37.

testimony of the presbyters, and it has to be established whether he used the term in a general way only as "the older men", the preceding generation, or whether he had in mind certain distinguished presbyters. It has been shown that the title of *presbyteros* had taken its origin from the members of the Jewish Sanhedrin.[1] In this sense it had been used as a self-description not only by St. Peter but also by the author of the second and third Epistles of St. John. Moreover, it had been employed for the Apostles themselves by Papias of Hierapolis. It appears from the careful collections of W. G. Manley that the term *presbyteros* was normally used in the early Church as one commanding respect, and an examination of the evidence from Irenaeus will confirm this view.[2]

Irenaeus referred to a presbyter or to presbyters as the authorities for his teaching. He fairly often referred to one particular "better man" (*kreisson*), and in one instance very impressively refers to "the presbyter, the disciple of the Apostles" who had instructed him in the significance of the existence of two Testaments, the Old and the New.[3] On the other hand, he also referred to a body of opinion, "the presbyters who were the disciples of the Apostles".[4] Such was his starting-point in his Demonstration of the Apostolic Preaching, where he also referred to such a group as being his authority for his teaching on the millennium. In his work against all heresies the same authority was again invoked, especially in the last two books. He said, for instance, that the presbyters had already proved "by reference to those who in olden times had disobeyed God, how insipid the men were who attempted to introduce another Father."[5] In all these cases the presbyters belonged to that generation which had received its instruction from the Apostles themselves.

[1] See above, chapter 1, p. 27.
[2] St. Peter, 1 Pet. 5: 1. 2 John 1; 3 John 1. Papias, Euseb., *H.E.* 3. 34. 3 ff.; cf. 36. 1. W. G. Manley, *On the Presbyterate* (1886).
[3] *Kreisson,* see Harvey's remarks 2. 238 n. 5. Two Testaments, *Adv. Haer.* 4. 49. 1 H. 2. 254.
[4] *Adv. Haer.* 5. 5. 1 H. 2. 331.
[5] Apostolic Preaching, *T.U.* 31 (1907), 3. Millennium, *ib.* 61, p. 35. Another Father, *Adv. Haer.* 4. 41. 1 H. 2. 244 ff.

As Irenaeus referred to them with regard to one particular point of doctrine, it is established that these presbyters were not a nebulous group of elders, but much rather a definite group. Moreover, it is possible to identify one at least of these presbyters, Polycarp, whose superior qualities were so strongly stressed in his Martyrium: "an Apostolic and prophetic teacher, having become bishop of the Catholic church at Smyrna."[1] Irenaeus himself, in his letter to Florinus, numbered him amongst "the presbyters who had planted together with the Apostles", and recorded how he had recollected his life with St. John and others who had seen the Lord.[2] Thus it appears that he was included among the presbyters, because he had been a man of exceptional qualities, an Apostolic man, who for this reason had already been put in charge by Ignatius of his desolate flock at Antioch.[3] In the case of Polycarp, therefore, the title of presbyter was used by Irenaeus as a title of honour, a usage which was also continued by others in later times. We find that Clement of Alexandria referred to his predecessor in the leadership of the catechetic school, Pantaenus, as "the presbyter", and Irenaeus himself, together with Papias of Hierapolis on the one hand, and Clement of Alexandria on the other, was referred to by Eusebius in a way similar to that in which he (Irenaeus) had frequently quoted the presbyters. It is therefore probable that in all the cases in which reference was made to an unspecified group of presbyters (a practice found, prior to Irenaeus, in Polycarp's *Epistle to the Philippians,* and continued on various occasions in Eusebius' *Ecclesiastical History,* long after Irenaeus) the persons envisaged were not just some elders, but persons of considerable and well-deserved authority, possessing exceptionally good information about the earliest teachings of the Church.[4]

From the special reverence paid to those presbyters it follows that their authority was invoked for a special purpose.

---

[1] *Acta Polyc.* 16. 1.
[2] Euseb., *H.E.* 5. 20. 4 ff.
[3] *Ib.* 3. 36. 10.
[4] Pantaenus, Euseb., *H.E.* 5. 4. 2; cf. 6. 13. 9; 14. 5. Irenaeus, *ib.* 5. 20. 1 ff. Papias, *ib.* 6. 13. 9. Polycarp, *Phil.* 9. 1. Presbyters, Euseb., *H.E.* 3. 3. 1; 3. 20. 9; 3. 24. 17; 5. 8. 1.

Irenaeus, being a scholar, was anxious to make sure of their support for his establishment of the Apostolic Creed and canon. He was prepared to accept this support, disregarding the question whether they had been bishops or not. In particular the men who were the authorities of Papias, Aristion and the presbyter John, and in later time the Alexandrians, Pantaenus and Clement, were not bishops. On the other hand, Irenaeus was not unmindful of the fact that the title of presbyter denoted a certain order in the Church hierarchy. After all, he himself had been a presbyter when the martyrs of Lyons had sent him to Pope Eleutherus of Rome. He also chose to contrast sinful, careless presbyters of his own time with that presbyterate "which guards the teaching of the Apostles and in the order of presbyter preserves pure preaching and an uncorrupt life." This saying makes it evident that some connotation of "Church dignitary" is to be understood when he refers to the authority of the presbyters; and the same emphasis appears even more when he challenges the heretics with the tradition which "comes from the Apostles and is observed by the presbyters within the churches". The plural "churches" not only indicates that he uses their official position as an argument, but it will be seen that it is in the same context that he makes his most important reference to the episcopal succession.[1]

Things were in a fluid state at that time, and the titles of *presbyteros* and in particular of *episcopos* were less clearly defined than they are now. In the Muratorian canon "fellow-disciples and -bishops" of St. John are mentioned, and although the reference is obscure it is most likely that, in view of the Roman origin of this source, they should be connected with the bishops mentioned twice in the plural by Hermas.[2] On the other hand, it is significant that Justin Martyr, whose evidence is particularly important for conditions at Rome, never mentioned bishops, but referred to the head of a Church as the *prohestos*, the president, a fact

[1] Quotations, *adv. Haer.* 4. 41. 1 H. 2. 237; *ib.* 3. 2. 2, followed immediately by the Roman succession list, *ib.* 3. 3. 2. Nevertheless, Harvey goes too far with his unqualified identification of presbyters and bishops.

[2] *Frg. Murat.* fol. 10, 10. Hermas, *Vis.*, 3. 5. 1; *Sim.* 9. 27. 2, cf. M. Dibelius, *Handb. Erg. Bd.* 634 ff.

which agrees well with the inscriptions on the earliest tombs
of Roman Popes, where the title of *episcopus* is not used before
the middle of the third century.[1] Under these circumstances
the following remark of Irenaeus deserves our most careful
inspection:

> Therefore obedience is due to those presbyters in the Church who,
> as we have shown, are in the succession after the Apostles, and who
> with their episcopal succession have received, according to the will
> of the Father a certain *charisma* of truth. (*Adv. Haer.* 4. 40. 2. H. 2. 236.)

This statement, which served as an introduction to his
attack upon the heretics *qui absistunt a principali successione*,[2]
consciously combined three elements: the *charisma* of truth,
which had been the prerogative of the prophets, as shown
in the preceding chapter, the Apostolic tradition through
the presbyters, and the Apostolic succession of the bishops.

These three elements taken together constitute the conception which Irenaeus connected with the Apostolic
succession, and it is evident that he was conscious of his
ingenious combination of the three. Perhaps the most elusive
of them is the "charismatic" element. An eminent Lutheran
historian, Karl Mueller, who was undoubtedly aware of the
passage just quoted, has nevertheless ventured to state:
"Irenaeus clearly nowhere speaks of a special *charisma* given
to the bishops on account of their ministry. If the bishops
are indeed of a special importance, as the successors of the
Apostles, this is so for two reasons which enable them to
continue the ministry of the Word: first, that their predecessors had received the truth from the Apostles; and
secondly that they, through their desire for truth and their
pure life, had been able to pass on the undefiled truth, so
that it was handed on from generation to generation."
Mueller has fortified this view by reference to Irenaeus'
pupil, Hippolytus, who violently denounced his adversary,

---

[1] Justin, cf. W. G. Manley, *Presbyterate* 44, whose remarks on Irenaeus, *ib.*
55 ff., should be read with caution. The "slow development of episcopacy out
of the presbyterate" is very doubtful; it is much rather a revolutionary development. Tombs of the Roman Popes, E. Friedberg, *Kirchenrecht*, 4th ed., 16 n. 62.

[2] Harvey, 2. 236 n. 3, translates *principalis* with *prohegoumenos*, giving it the
meaning of "more ancient", but it means just like *principalitas* in 3. 3. 1, also
the supremacy of rank.

H

Pope Callistus, for holding that a bishop, even if he had committed a deadly sin, could not be deposed.[1]

It seems that the passage quoted above has been seen by Mueller in the light of another, from which it is only separated by the chapter *De Presbyteris Iniustis*:

> For where the *charismata* of the Lord abide, there the truth should be learned, i.e. from those who have the ecclesiastical succession after the Apostles, and all that constitutes a wholesome conduct of life in the unchangeable and incorruptible Logos.[2] (*Adv. Haer.* 4. 42. 1. H. 2, 238.)

If it is assumed that the average clergy were utterly corrupt and that only those exceptional bishops who conformed to such a very high moral standard as this were endowed with the *charismata* of the Lord, Mueller's conclusion would be inevitable. Such a view, however, is incompatible with the confident assurance given elsewhere by Irenaeus, "innumerable are the *charismata* which the Church dispenses throughout the world, having received them from God . . . without deception or charge to anybody." He obviously believed that it was the rule rather than the exception among the clergy to follow Moses, Samuel, and St. Paul, whom he set up as examples at the end of the chapter *De Presbyteris Iniustis*. The problem of the *character indelebilis* of the episcopacy was not touched upon by Irenaeus, and it may be regarded as unmethodical to discuss it in this connexion. It is at least certain that the ministers of a blameless conduct were endowed with the Divine *charismata* and distributed their fruits among men, without ever exhausting them.[3]

With regard to the Apostolic tradition it has to be said that Irenaeus in addition to his polemical purpose was

[1] K. Mueller, *Z.N.W.* 23 (1924), 219. Hippol., *Philos.* 9. 12. 21 ff. *Werke* 3. 249. 21 ff.

[2] In the last clause I have regarded Latin *conversatio* and *sermo* as the equivalents of Greek *politeia* and *Logos*, and fashioned the English translation accordingly.

[3] *Charismata, Adv. Haer.* 2. 49. 3 H. 1. 375. Moses, etc., *ib.* 4. 41. 2 H. 2. 237 ff. *Character indelebilis:* it should be certain, in spite of inscriptions like *C.I.G.* 9259, mentioning a *dis presbyteros*, that Harnack, *Kirchenverf.* 69 n. 1, is right that nobody from the second century onwards contested the life-long appointment of the clergy, unless they were convicted of deadly sins. The earliest theological statement on the *character indelebilis* of the priesthood is found in Augustine, *De Bono Coniugali* 37; cf. E. Friedberg, *op. cit.*, 23 n. 11. The case Cyprian versus Stephen of Rome has no such statement.

inspired by a scholarly interest in the genealogy of the Christian doctrine, which was largely historical and purely human. In this he followed the example of other scholars of his age. A similar interest inspired Diogenes Laertius to compile his collection of Lives of the Philosophers, and Philostratus his Lives of the Sophists. Schools and the succession of their various heads were discussed also among lawyers and physicians, in short by all those who had a good—Hellenistic—education. A type of succession was evolved which not only rejoiced in the greatness of the leaders of previous generations but also recorded their failings.[1] Eusebius, who, a century later, recorded anecdotes of Narcissus of Jerusalem in this vein, used terms characteristic of Irenaeus when he said that they had come to him "by the tradition and succession" after Narcissus.[2] This shows that Irenaeus' concept of the succession of the presbyters, the Apostolic tradition, was germane to the general interest mentioned.

In the case of one of the presbyters of Irenaeus, Papias of Hierapolis, we may go even further. Eusebius[3] characterized him as "having been of a very small mind, when judged by his own words, yet he became an authority for many churchmen after him, who agreed with him because of his eldership, as for instance Irenaeus and those who accept his views." This outburst was directed against the millennarianism of Papias, for in the following paragraphs Eusebius quite unblushingly accepted his authority on the authorship of the four canonical Gospels. Under these conditions we may well surmise that he himself was not the first to voice such temperamental criticism. Irenaeus had also used the authority of Papias on the authorship of the Gospels without reference to his source.[4] In his exposition of the millennarian doctrine, on the other hand, he quoted him by name in one instance (5. 33. 4), and it is certain that his

---

[1] The piquancy of Pliny's anecdote about the distraction, if not worse, of Javolenus, *Ep.* 6. 15, was tremendously increased by the fact that its object was the head of the famous law school of the *Sabiniani*.

[2] *H.E.* 6. 9. 1 ff.

[3] *Ib.* 3. 39. 13; cf. also the preceding paragraph on the millennium.

[4] Canonical Gospels, Euseb., *H.E.* 3. 39. 14 ff.; Iren., *adv. Haer.* 3. 1. 2, cf. Harvey, 2. 2 n. 4.

influence may be felt in other contexts as well, even where nothing is to be found but a general reference to "the presbyters".[1] Now, Irenaeus begins the series of chapters that lead up to the doctrine of the Anti-Christ and the millennium with a spirited attack upon those who "relinquish the teaching of the Church and accuse the holy elders of ignorance, not realizing how much more there is to a devout ordinary Christian than to a blasphemous and impudent Sophist."[2] This suggests strongly that he was already faced with attacks upon Papias similar to that of Eusebius, but it proves still more. It shows that the idea of school traditions was in the mind of Irenaeus—and probably his adversaries—when he countered their accusation of insufficient insight by his reference to the power of faith. Christian tradition could be validly upheld by a *religiosus idiota*, whereas the tradition of the schools of the sophists could not.

The guarantee of this was the ministerial succession in the Church. It has been mentioned that Irenaeus was aware that the idea of Church dignitary was implicit when he referred to "the presbyters". It will now be shown that he used it on purpose. Papias, so Eusebius informs us,[3] frequently quoted his authorities, Aristion and the presbyter John, by name, and it would have been easy, and in no way contrary to the standards of contemporary scholarship, for Irenaeus to quote them by name on Papias' authority. However, as persons they were already half-forgotten, and we may doubt whether their fame had ever reached the readers of Irenaeus' treatise. It was their standing as presbyters of the Church which commanded respect.

This respect for the ministry of the presbyters was strengthened by its identification with the episcopacy. It has been seen that the close relation between the two titles dated back to Apostolic times, the church officers at Ephesus being described alternately as presbyters in Acts 20: 17 and

[1] Harvey, 2. 417 n. 3, has shown this, commenting on *adv. Haer.* 5. 33. 3. Perhaps the same applies to the exegesis of the Sower, Matt. 13: 8, in *adv. Haer.* 5. 36. 1 H. 2. 427 ff., and its parallels, Cyprian, *Hab. Virg.* 21 Hartel 202; Ps. Cyprian, *De Centesima*, ed. R. Reitzenstein, *Z.N.W.*, 15 (1914), 61 ff.; cf. H. Koch, *ib.* 31 (1932), 248 ff. It would be a prime example of the "strange interpretations" of Christ's parables ascribed to Papias, Euseb., *H.E.* 3. 39. 11.
[2] Iren., *adv. Haer.* 5. 20. 2 H. 2. 379.
[3] *H.E.* 3. 39. 7; cf. 14.

as bishops in Acts 20: 28; but Irenaeus makes it clear that there was no unbroken continuation of that usage. For in his interpretation of Acts 20: 28[1] he did not explain the plurality of bishops mentioned there by a reference to the plurality of presbyters mentioned in verse 17, but maintained, in contradiction to the evidence from Acts, that St. Paul had summoned to Miletus bishops and presbyters "who were from Ephesus and the cities around". Mon-episcopacy was well on its way, and the title of *episcopos* for the head of the Church in the cities of Asia Minor was so common that a plurality of bishops in an individual town there was unheard of in the time of Irenaeus.[2]

It was in Rome that the identification of the titles of presbyter and bishop was still easy. Irenaeus in his letter to Pope Victor I on the question of the date of Easter plainly referred to the earlier Popes as presbyters: "the presbyters before Soter, the leaders of the Church of which you now have the cure, Anicetus I mean, and Pius, Hyginus, Telesphorus, Sixtus", etc.[3] On the other hand, it may be seen from Irenaeus' introduction to his list of the Roman Popes[4] that he did not only state in general that "the tradition of the Apostles, made manifest throughout the world, may be inspected by all the seekers of the truth, for we can enumerate the *episcopi* appointed by the Apostles and their successions down to our time", he even added a specific statement with regard to Rome:

as it would be rather tedious to set out in a book like this[5] the successions in all the churches, we will give a summary of the Apostolic tradition of the greatest and most generally known Church of Rome, which was founded and organized by the most glorious Apostles Peter and Paul, and holds it through the succession of bishops unto our own time.

Just as in the passage from which we have started, 4. 40. 2,

[1] *Adv. Haer.* 3. 14. 2 H. 2. 76.

[2] An interesting illustration of the fact that the system of a plurality of bishops was localized in the West comes from Theodore of Mopsuestia, *Comm.* 1 *Tim.*, ed. Swete (1882), 2. 121 ff., cf. Harnack, *Mission*, 4th ed., 1. 459 ff.

[3] Euseb., *H.E.* 5. 24. 14. I hesitate to connect this with the fact that Apollinarius of Hierapolis described Zoticus of Otrys in Phrygia as presbyter, calling himself *sympresbyteros*, Euseb., *H.E.* 5. 16. 5. This is a genuine parallel to 1 Pet. 5. 1, although no other similarity to this verse is found in the passage.

[4] *Adv. Haer.* 3. 3. 1 H. 2. 8 ff.

[5] *In hoc tali volumine*, in a book like this, makes reference to Hegesippus, the authority of Irenaeus, who had been concerned with "very many bishops", Euseb., *H.E.* 4. 22. 1, establishing several Apostolic successions, *ib.* 4. 8. 1.

the succession of presbyters is alternatively described as an episcopal succession, so it is with regard to the Roman succession, the only difference being that the two do not appear in one and the same passage, but in two different relics of Irenaeus' literary work.[1]

It is possible that Irenaeus was more keenly interested in the Roman succession, because he was more closely connected with the Roman Church than with any other. In Hegesippus' book he had at his disposal succession lists of several Churches, and it is significant that he chose the Roman list. The first and undisputed reason for this was the local connexion with Rome, which was the Apostolic see in the West. For even if St. Paul, as the *Vercelli Acts* and the *Muratorian Canon* suggest,[2] had journeyed to Spain, no record of any succession after him had been established in that country. Irenaeus could say, like Tertullian, *si autem Italia adiaces, habes Romam, unde nobis quoque auctoritas praesto est.* This was certainly implied in his praise of the Roman Church, *ad hanc enim ecclesiam propter potentiorem principalitatem necesse est omnem convenire ecclesiam, hoc est eos qui undique sunt fideles.*[3] Tertullian's saying and probably also that of Irenaeus led to a second principle, that of mother- and daughter-churches. Tertullian stated quite clearly, "churches which cannot name an Apostle or any Apostolic man as their founder, because they are more recent, being founded every day even now, are regarded as being no less Apostolic because of the identity of their teaching."[4] In the case of Irenaeus the connexion with Rome may have been closer still. It is well known that at about this time bishop Demetrius of Alexandria created the first three Catholic bishops in the provincial towns of Egypt. In the *Doctrina Addai* the fact is mentioned that Palut was consecrated by Sarapion of

---

[1] If the Roman Popes could be described as presbyters, the proof of Dom G. Dix, *Ap. Trad.* xxviii ff., that Hippolytus was denied episcopal rank, when his followers rejoined the Church after his martyrdom, is put in jeopardy. For it hinges upon the description of Hippolytus as presbyter in the Liberian catalogue and later documents. The authors of these documents may not have seen him as bishop, but his contemporaries may have thought differently.

[2] *Vercelli Acts* 1, M. R. James, *Apocr. N.T.* (1926) 304; *Frag. Mur.* fol. 10 b, 38 ff.

[3] Tert., *Praescr. Haer.* 36. Iren., *Adv. Haer.* 3. 3. 1 H. 2. 9.

[4] Tert., *op. cit.*, 32 fin.

Antioch to the see of Edessa, ultimately deriving his succession from Zephyrinus of Rome. Finally, Hippolytus of Rome in his *Apostolic Tradition* demands that a bishop should be consecrated by at least two other bishops. From these analogies we venture to conclude that Irenaeus, who had been sent to Rome as a presbyter and returned to Lyons to be the successor of the martyr bishop Pothinus, was consecrated at the hands of Pope Eleutherus.[1]

In addition to the local and personal connexion with Rome, Irenaeus in his choice of the Roman succession as prototype was the first Father of the Church to state the primacy of Rome.[2] It is essential to realize that he referred to two more Churches, the Church of Smyrna and the Church of Ephesus. A comparison between the two references to Rome and Smyrna—Ephesus is only just mentioned —gives an excellent illustration of the difference between the Apostolic succession and tradition. Smyrna had the tradition of Polycarp, the pupil of the Apostles; and his successors counted for so little that Irenaeus did not even mention their names. Rome, on the other hand, used the Apostolic authority as a Church, and Irenaeus even credited I *Clement* to the whole Roman Church and not to Clement of Rome personally, suppressing the witness of Philippians 4: 3 to the name of Clement.[3] Two systems of Apostolic attestation thus appear once more at the root of Irenaeus' conception of the Apostolic tradition and succession.

[1] Demetrius, cf. Harnack, *Mission*, 4th ed., I. 472; W. Bauer, *Rechtglaeubigkeit und Ketzerei* (1934) 57; G. Krueger, *Handb.*, 2nd ed., 110. Hippol., *Ap. Trad.* 2. 3, but the case is not quite certain, because the Latin omits *episcopi*. Consecration of Irenaeus, Euseb., *H.E.* 5. 5. 8, makes no explicit mention of it, but the change from 5. 1. 29, Pothinus being "entrusted" with the see, to which Irenaeus "succeeded", may have a hidden meaning. The doubts expressed by E. Molland, *J.E.H.* I (1950), 27, as to the consecration of Irenaeus are perhaps not sufficiently substantiated: when the martyrs wrote their letter of recommendation, bishop Pothinus may still have been alive. The real difficulty lies in the election of Irenaeus. Was there a body of Christians left at Lyons by which he could be elected? On the relations between mother- and daughter-churches cf. K. Mueller, *Abh. Berlin* (1922) 3. 33 ff.

[2] Not of the Roman bishop. This difference must always be kept in mind in any discussion with Rome, cf. F. W. Puller, *Primitive Saints*, 3rd ed. (1900), 34 ff.

[3] *Adv. Haer.* 3. 3. 3–4 H. 2. 10 ff. The fact that Irenaeus knew Philippians follows from his knowledge of Marcion's *Apostolus*, but Harvey's Index shows that he used this Epistle very sparingly.

It has been suggested that the system of Apostolic tradition needed to be reinforced by that of Apostolic succession.[1] This contention will serve only when it is shown from whence the power of the latter system was derived. German scholars are inclined to attribute a daemonic character to the "political genius" and the "will to power" of Rome. Rudolf Sohm was neither the first nor the last to refer to these two as the supreme causes of the decline of the Apostolic Church. The Roman list of bishops, being the earliest of its kind that still exists, has led them to accept the Roman origin of the idea of the Apostolic succession.[2] By many others it has been seen as yet another clever move on the chess-board of Church politics. We ask, however, how and why did this move influence Rome's adversaries, or, more specifically—for we do not believe in the Roman origin of the doctrine—what was the compelling force behind the idea of an Apostolic succession of bishops? To answer this question we turn once more to *Adv. Haer.* 4. 40. 2, in order to show that there really was such a compelling force: "therefore it is necessary to obey the presbyters who . . . have received the Apostolic succession and by their episcopal succession have received the *charisma* of truth."

The idea of obedience to the bishops arose from the commands of St. Paul (1 Cor. 16: 16; 1 Thess. 5: 12 ff.), and especially from Hebrews 13: 17, which seems to have been in Irenaeus' mind. It was not, therefore, a Roman invention, but had its ultimate source in the command to obey the priests and Levites (Deut. 17: 10 ff.). This is shown by the fact that a similar command was enforced with the same vigour in the Jewish synagogue.[3] It is true that in the Roman Church 1 *Clement* 1. 3; 21. 6 repeated this command very impressively, but non-Roman Fathers did the same, and the earliest exposition of this duty in all its aspects is found in the pseudo-Clementine Homilies. Here Zacchaeus, the

[1] W. Bauer, *Rechtglaeubigkeit* 122 ff.

[2] R. Sohm, *Kirchenrecht* 1. 214 n. 10, with reference to Harnack, *Dogmen-Gesch.* 1. 402. Similar views in W. Bauer, *loc. cit.*, E. Caspar, *Papst-Gesch.* 1. 10 ff., is more cautious, cf. esp. 10 n. 4, where he connects the Roman succession list with its Islamic counterparts.

[3] Cf. H. Windisch, *Herbraeer-Brief*, 2nd ed. (1931), 119 ff., with ample references not only to the synagogue but also to the early Fathers.

bishop to be, objected to the title of *archon,* prince or ruler,
although St. Peter is portrayed as employing all the arguments in favour of it which could be drawn from second-
century monarchianism—and eventually obtained permis-
sion to be called *cathestos,* the appointed minister. St. Peter
scored, however, in the end, by commanding the congregation to treat Zacchaeus as their *archon.*[1] The reason for
this dispute was the Old Testament witness for the episcopacy (Is. 60: 17): "I shall give thee thy *archontes* in peace
and thy *episcopoi* in righteousness." This passage, which
*1 Clement* 44. 3 had already used in a somewhat expurgated
form, was also used by Irenaeus—in its unadulterated form—
*dabo tibi principes tuos in pace et episcopos tuos in iustitia.*[2] He was
the second Roman witness to the use of this testimony, the
third being Hippolytus (*Ap. Trad.* 3. 2) *principes et sacerdotes
constituens,* who made it clear that all these references had
for their source the Roman consecration ritual.[3] These
sayings indicate a strong Old Testament influence as well as
commands akin to those of the Synagogue, two constituents
which appear to have been less powerful in Tertullian and
in the early western Church Orders.[4]

Obedience to the bishop was demanded because of his
priesthood, and in this respect Irenaeus showed his obligation to the Old Testament still more clearly. Irenaeus,
it seems, started from the doctrine of a general priesthood
of all believers, as will be seen from the following quotation,
"we have shown in the previous book that all the disciples
of the Lord are Levites and priests."[5] The same starting-

[1] Zacchaeus, *Hom.* 3. 61 Lag. 53. 10 ff. Monarchianism, *ib.* 62 Lag. 53. 15 ff.;
cf. E. Peterson, *Monotheismus* (1934) 122. *Cathestos, ib.* 64 Lag. 53. 21 ff., cf.
the use of *prohestos* for the bishop in Justin Martyr, and the *prohistamenos* in
1 Thess. 5: 12. There seems to have been a deep-rooted objection to the use
of the title of *archon* in the early Church. Admonition to obey, *Hom.* 3. 67 Lag.
54. 24 ff., cf. *ib.* 11. 36 Lag. 120. 15 ff., where a similar admonition is administered at the consecration of Maroones of Tripolis, and *Const. Apost.* 7. 9. 1.
[2] *Adv. Haer.* 4. 41. 2 H. 2. 238.
[3] Dom G. Dix in his edition of this as well as in the *Apostolic Ministry* has
ignored the allusion.
[4] Tertullian, *Exhort. Cast.* 7. Church Order, *Statt. Eccl. Ant.* c. 35 Bruns 1. 145,
*ut episcopus in ecclesia et in consessu presbyterorum sublimior sedeat; intra domo vero
collegam se presbyterorum cognoscat.* Compare with this the parallel in *Didasc. Syr.*
2. 57. 2, which is under the influence of the Ps. Clementines.
[5] *Adv. Haer.* 5. 34. 3 H. 2. 422; cf. *ib.* 4. 17. 1 H. 2. 168.

point, of which the New Testament basis is 1 Peter 2: 5; 9, was even chosen for his momentous statement on the priesthood of the Apostles:

> For every just man is of the sacerdotal order.[1] Therefore are priests all the Apostles of the Lord, who have inherited neither lands nor houses, but always minister to the altar of the Lord. (*Adv. Haer.* 4. 17. 1. H. 2. 167 ff.)

And he fortified his thesis by Moses' benediction of Levi (Deut. 33: 9): "who said to his father and mother, I have not seen you; neither did he acknowledge his brethren, nor knew his own children: for he has observed thy commandments and kept thy covenant."

There is no express statement in Irenaeus that the bishops and presbyters of the Church continued the Old Testament priesthood; his idea was that of representation rather than of continuation: "for in the same way in which we were foreshadowed and announced in the people of the First Covenant, so also are they depicted in us, i.e. in the Church, and receive their reward for their labours."[2] However, it can be shown that his idea was no more than a necessary reform of the idea of continuation as found for instance in 1 *Clement* 41; 43, where the elements of the idea are all to be found. There is the tremendous respect for the primitive Church at Jerusalem: "these are the words of the Church from which every church has its origin, the words of the metropolis of the citizens of the New Covenant."[3] There is the Roman succession list, adopted from Hegesippus and strongly resembling the succession list of the Jewish High Priests, as has been shown above in the second chapter. There is the reference to Isaiah 60: 17, which in 1 *Clement* 44. 3 was closely bound up with the doctrine that the priest in the Church continued the priesthood of Israel. Finally, there is the unfavourable reference to the *traditiones presbyterorum*, the rules of the Jewish Sanhedrin, enlarging the Mosaic Law, and using the title of presbyter with the

---

[1] I have a strong suspicion that the "kings" added by the Greek are of Byzantine origin.
[2] *Adv. Haer.* 4. 36. 2 H. 2. 299.
[3] *Ib.* 3. 12. 6 H. 2. 58.

same connotation of the ministry as in the case of "the presbyters".[1]

This close analogy between the Old Testament and the Christian priesthood formed the backbone of Irenaeus' resistance to the gnostic heresy. The gnostic doctrines had sprung from the mixture of religious elements to which true Judaism was both consciously and subconsciously opposed, in spite of the fact that Gnosticism had incorporated various strong elements of oriental and even sometimes of Jewish origin. Irenaeus opposed them by claiming that "true gnosis is the teaching of the Apostles and the old-established Church throughout all the world, and the character of the body of Christ, according to the succession of bishops, to whom the Apostles entrusted the Church universal." For all the Gnostics had been "ever so much later than the bishops to whom the Apostles had entrusted the Church."[2]

The polemical purpose of Irenaeus' work made him insist upon the fact that the Apostolic succession of the bishops included also the succession to their *magisterium*. They had to set an example, and therefore they had an increased responsibility with regard to the whole conduct of their lives. For the good ministers a great reward is in store, and for the bad a *magna calamitas*.[3] There is little doubt that Irenaeus wrote his chapter *De Presbyteris Iniustis* (4. 41) with reference to the unfaithful presbyters of the Church, but that was not his sole purpose. For the Gnostics also referred to Apostolic traditions, as we have already seen,[4] and there even arose among them something similar to the succession of the presbyters in the list of the Samaritan Gnostics, Simon Magus, Dositheus, and Menander. We may even see in the competition between the lists originating from Jerusalem and Hegesippus on the one hand, and

---

[1] *Ib.* 4. 23. 1 H. 2. 179. The Latin usually calls the Jewish Elders by the name of *seniores*. The translator may have found the analogy too close for his liking.

[2] True gnosis, *adv. Haer.* 4. 53. 2 H. 2. 262 ff. Gnostics, *ib.* 5. 20. 1 H. 2. 377 ff.

[3] *Adv. Haer.* 3. 3. 1 H. 2. 9.

[4] In Egypt in particular there seems to have been a competition for the sponsorship of the Twelve, Clem. Alex., *Ecl.* 16, called them "saviours"; Origen, *Hom. Num.* 12. 2, "kings"; the *Pistis Sophia* c. 7 (Schmidt), "saviours"; cf. Harnack, *Mission*, 4th ed., 1. 361 n.

from Samaria on the other, a last spark of the age-old
conflict between the two religious centres on Mount Sion
and Mount Gerizim.[1] All this was taken up in Irenaeus'
doctrine of the Apostolic tradition and succession; yet his
strongest conviction, however difficult it may be to describe,
was that it was a succession in the Divine Spirit: "for where
the Church is, there is the Spirit of God; and where the
Spirit of God is, there is the Church and all grace: and the
Spirit is truth."[2]

Whoever may have started these theories of which
Irenaeus was hardly the originator, it is certain that the
two great theologians of the Western Church who may be
regarded as his disciples, Hippolytus and Tertullian,
exhibited very similar ideas about the Christian ministry,
and therefore may be regarded as having been under his
influence in this respect. In the case of Hippolytus, there is
one very pertinent remark to be found in the introduction
to his *Philosophumena*.[3] There he refers to "the Holy Spirit
whom the Apostles have received and handed on to the
orthodox believers. We, having become their successors,
have part in the same benefice of the High Priesthood and
ministry of the Word (*didaskalia*) and have been chosen
watchmen of the Church." These words, which are remi-
niscent of the theory of Irenaeus—namely, that the bishops
had succeeded in particular to the teaching duties (*magisterium*) of the Apostles—represent a view which became
popular in Rome during this time. They are closely akin
to the claims put forward by the author of pseudo-Cyprian's
*De Aleatoribus*, in the first chapter of his otherwise rather
insignificant pamphlet.[4] There seems to be good reason to
believe that this work was written in the second half of the
third century by a Novatianist, schismatic bishop of Rome;
and the similarity lends colour to the erroneous Roman

[1] Euseb., *H.E.* 4. 22. 5, cf. *ib.* 3. 26. 1.
[2] *Adv. Haer.* 3. 38. 1 H. 2. 132.
[3] Hippol., *Philos.* 1 pr. 6 *Werke* 3. 3. 1 ff.
[4] Ps. Cyprian, *Aleat.* 1 Hartel 92 ff., *et quoniam in nobis Divina et paterna pietas
apostolatus ducatum contulit et vicariam Domini sedem caelesti dignatione ordinavit, et
originem authentici apostolatus super quem Christus fundavit ecclesiam in superiore
nostro portamus, accepta simul potestate ligandi et curatione peccata dimittendi: salutari
doctrina admonimur ne, dum delinquentibus adsidue ignoscimus, ipsi cum eis pariter
torqueamur.*

tradition which connected Hippolytus with the schism of Novatian, although he died a martyr's death almost twenty years before Novatianism came into existence.[1] The expression of those views was not, however, reserved for schismatics. Similar claims seem to have been promoted also by the Catholic Pope of Rome, and it is possible to see here the unfavourable reaction among the African Montanists. For the ironical way in which Tertullian in *De Pudicitia* addressed Pope Callistus as *apostolice*[2] must refer to a statement similar to the two former, which transgressed the limits of the Apostolic succession drawn by Irenaeus' theory. Irenaeus had represented the earlier Popes as comparable to the "Apostolic" presbyters of the type of Polycarp and Papias. Tertullian vainly resisted the extension of this quality to the ruling Pope.[3]

Apart from the introduction to the *Philosophumena*, no sayings of Hippolytus can be quoted which directly support the theory of the Apostolic succession. There are only sidelights thrown upon it in the first place by the title of his Treatise on the Apostolic Tradition. It may be taken for granted that this Church Order would not bear the title by which it is known to-day had it not been for Irenaeus' combination of the ideas of the Apostolic tradition and succession. This is fully brought out, if we may assume— as indeed we must—that the title which we find inscribed upon Hippolytus' statue is correct — περὶ χαρισμάτων ἀποστολικὴ παράδοσις, the Apostolic tradition concerning the *charismata*, the ministries of the Church.[4] For it has been shown how Irenaeus insisted upon the "charismatic" character of the episcopacy. Much less important are the contents of the book itself. There is only one rule which has any bearing on the doctrine of the Apostolic succession, that which prescribes that a new bishop should be consecrated by the laying on of hands of several bishops.[5] This

---

[1] Hippol., *Ap.Trad.*, ed. Dix, p. xxviii ff.; xxxii ff.

[2] Tert., *Pudic.* 21.

[3] On Tertullian's adversary, I have accepted the views of A. d'Alès, *L'Edit de Calliste* (1914).

[4] E. Caspar, *Gesch. d. Papsttums* 1. 30. Dom G. Dix, although he mentions the inscription, does not discuss it, but tacitly accepts on p. lxxi the view that there was a separate treatise *On the Charismata* by Hippolytus, which is unlikely.

[5] *Ap. Trad.* 2. 3, but notice that the crucial word *episcopi* is missing from the Latin version.

practice was not general: in the Life of Gregory Thaumatur-
gus by Gregory of Nyssa it still appears that the Saint by
himself was sufficient to consecrate the bishops whom he
created, and in Origen's description of the foundation of an
Eastern Church, *Hom. Num.* 11. 4, no mention is made of the
consecration of the first bishop.[1] Under these circumstances
it seems wise to regard Hippolytus' statement as evidence
for conditions obtaining only in Italy at the end of the
second century.[2] An indirect light is thrown by Hippolytus
upon the priesthood of the bishops in his remarks on the
conflict between the High Priesthood of Jesus on the one
hand, and that of Annas and Caiaphas on the other.[3] For
Hippolytus in the *Philosophumena* had clearly described
himself as High Priest after the Apostles. Here, therefore,
Hippolytus laid his finger on the very place from which
the priesthood of the Church takes its origin. There is,
finally, a saying of doubtful origin and ambiguous meaning
in the fragments of Hippolytus' *Theophaneia*. It contains the
following command of the Lord, given to St. John the
Baptist: "Baptize me, O John, that no one may hold baptism
in contempt. For by you, who are my servant, I am baptized,
so that in future no king or governor may disdain to be
baptized by a beggarly priest."[4] This might be taken as an
indication of the dependence of the priesthood of the
Christian Church upon the ancient prophetic ministry;
but it seems that the sentiment voiced is more germane to
the views of later centuries.

If the evidence from Hippolytus is not very great, that
from Tertullian is all the more comprehensive. The basis of
his argument appears in his attack upon the Roman Church
in *Adversus Praxeam* where he propounded an elaborate

[1] The witness of the *Testamentum Domini* to an early origin of the consecration
rite in the East is hardly admissible, unless the objections are refuted which were
raised by A. Baumstark, *Roem. Quart. Schr.* 14 (1900), 1 ff.

[2] Dom G. Dix, *Apostolic Ministry* 193, adding "everywhere" to *Ap. Trad.*,
intr. 2, and "in the second century" to his quotation from Harnack, has taken
a dangerous course. Both these points deserve a most careful examination, and
the apparent justification of the first by the subsequent reception of the *Ap.
Trad.* in the East (when? where? excepting Egypt) may prove no closer affinity
of actual conditions than the reception of the Swiss Civil Code in Turkey.

[3] *Benedict. Jacob.*, ed. Diobouniotis-Beis (*T.U.* 38, 1911) 31. 24 ff.

[4] *Theoph.*, ch. 5, *Werke* 1. 2. 260. 8 ff.

formula of the Creed, of which he said that it was derived
from the Gospels "long before all heresies, let alone that of
Praxeas, which is only of yesterday". Tertullian's remark
thus contains a reference to the Apostolic tradition of the
Creed which could not be misunderstood by his Roman
adversaries.[1] Starting from this point, his various sayings
may be arranged in a systematic order. First, he maintained
that "Jesus Christ is the Catholic Priest of the Father".
Subsequently, he expressed his view of the significance of the
Apostolate of the Twelve, the commissioning of whom had
been prophesied in the Old Testament.[2] With regard to
the Apostolate of St. Paul, however, he entered into an
argument with Marcion, of whom he demanded evidence
from the Old Testament as well as from the Acts of the
Apostles, because St. Paul's name was not found *in albo
Apostolorum*, in the Gospels. Here the Jewish-Christian
prejudice against the Apostle of the Gentiles reappears, but
it is not to be treated wholly as the clever ruse of a trained
advocate, although Tertullian in another context calmly
called a ruling of St. Paul's "that tradition of the Apostles
which is held sacred in the churches of the Apostles."[3] It
is none the less true that the use of the Pauline Epistles alone,
when severed from their connexion with the other Apostolic
writings and from the Old Testament, had proved to be
one of the strongest sources of Christian Gnosticism.

Tertullian argued that the Apostles had been made the
stewards of the divine household, and to them and "to all
who were going to be at the head of churches" Christ had
given His warning with regard to their stewardship in the
parable of the faithful and the unfaithful steward, Luke
12: 40 ff.[4] Let the heretics prove their succession after the
Apostles or, at least, after those Apostolic men who had been
in constant communion with the Apostles—perhaps an
allusion to a succession like that after St. Mark at Alexandria.
"Let them therefore show the origins of their churches, let

[1] Creed, *adv. Prax.* 2; cf. *Praescr.* 13; 36; *Apol.* 18, and Hahn-Harnack,
*Bibliothek d. Symbole*, 3rd ed. (1897), 9 ff.
[2] Catholic Priest, *adv. Marc.* 4. 9. The Twelve, *ib.* 4. 13.
[3] St. Paul, *adv. Marc.* 5. 1, the *album* being the register of the jurors in a Roman
court. Tradition of the Apostles and St. Paul, *ib.* 4. 5.
[4] *Adv. Marc.* 4. 29.

them produce the lists of their bishops, so that their first
bishop is shown to have been instituted or preceded by an
Apostle or an Apostolic man."¹ Tertullian shows by this
demand that the theory of the succession of the Gnostics had
aroused the attention of the Christian theologians from
among the Gentiles. He also makes it clear that he was aware
of the difference between the Apostles and the bishops,
although his saying leaves open the possibility that an
Apostle might have become the bishop of a church, a
tradition connected, so it seems, with the Apostle St. John
at Ephesus.² Tertullian also stated quite plainly that the
Apostolic succession was the continuation of the Levitical
priesthood.³ On the other hand, it was an episcopal succession; even the heretics were challenged to produce their lists
of bishops. But above all it was the succession to the ministry
of the Word, the Apostolic doctrine. "For the preaching of
the disciples may become suspect because of their ambition,
if it is not assisted by the authority of their teachers." The
administration of the Sacraments, Eucharist and Baptism,
which had been open to everyone in the African Church,
was entrusted to the bishops only, so Tertullian says, by
ecclesiastical custom, in a spirit of deferential submission.⁴

It is significant how, from these presuppositions, which
already were becoming slightly antiquated, Tertullian
resisted the claim that the bishop possessed the right to
forgive the sin of fornication, made by Pope Callistus, that
"good shepherd and blessed Father, who counts his goats
for his sheep". Tertullian granted to the bishop no more than
the right of forgiving venial offences; whereas deadly sins,
if committed after baptism, could only be forgiven by God
Himself. This was true even in the case of the Roman Church,
the blood relation of St. Peter, who had been granted by the
Lord Himself the privilege of binding and unbinding. "For
in accordance with the personality of Peter, such a privilege
belongs to a spiritual man, Apostle or prophet. For the

¹ Apostles and Apostolic men, *Praescr. Haer.* 32.
² Cf. Polycrates in Euseb., *H.E.* 3. 31. 3, "who was made priest, wearing
the diadem".
³ *Adv. Marc.* 4. 23 fin; *Monog.* 7.
⁴ Ministry of the Word, *adv. Marc.* 4. 2; cf. *ib.* 1. 21. Eucharist, *Corona* 3.
Baptism, *Bapt.* 17.

Church is really and primarily the Spirit Himself in whom is the Trinity of the One Godhead, Father, Son, and Holy Ghost. . . . Therefore the Church will forgive sins, but that is the Church of the Spirit through a spiritual man, not the Church of the synod of bishops."[1] The jealousy between bishops and prophets loomed large once more in this Montanist proclamation. The possibility of such an attitude was created by the peculiar conditions within the African Church, where the distinction between clergy and laity was still recent, and, as yet, somewhat vague and undefined. There were women seated with the *ordo* of presbyters in the chancel, and although Tertullian admitted that the clergy were the *ordo sacerdotalis*, he nevertheless insisted upon adding that "only the authority of the Church had created the distinction between clergy and laity, and only by the sitting together [of the clergy] had the distinction assumed sanctity."[2] He therefore felt that it was in order to compare the Christian clergy with the secular authority: "let the Senate blush, and all the other orders, let them blush too"; these were words addressed to the Christian presbyters and the other clergy.[3]

The whole clergy seems to have comprised four orders—bishop, presbyters, deacons, and widows—and probably no more. Of these orders only the bishop, unless he commissioned one of the other men—but never a woman—was allowed to baptize and to celebrate the Eucharist. In cases of emergency, however, persecution or plague, when unfortunately the clergy did not invariably stay at their posts, lay people were still allowed to administer either of these Sacraments. Tertullian's greatest argument for the monogamy of all Christian people was just this, that anyone might be called upon to perform the duties of a Christian priest who, by the rule of the Pastoral Epistles, had to be "the husband of one wife". The emergency administration

---

[1] Good shepherd, *Pud.* 13. Venial offences, *ib.* 18. *Petri propinqua, ib.* 21, cf. W. Koehler, *S.B.,* Heidelberg (1938). Spiritual man, *ib.* 21 fin. Tertullian, who wrote this as a Montanist, ostensibly referred to 1 Cor. 2: 13 ff., but in reality he meant, of course, Montanus and his prophetesses.

[2] Women sitting amongst the *ordo, ad Ux.* 1. 7 *viduas adlegi in ordinem,* cf. K. Mueller, *Z.N.W.* 28 (1929) 275 esp. *ib.* n. 2. *Ordo sacerdotalis, Exhort. Cast.* 7, constituted by the authority of the Church, *ib.*

[3] Secular authorities, *Spect.* 17.

of the Sacraments was also used as an effective barrier against the claim *omnia licet episcopis,* which was heard already at this early stage of the struggle of the bishops against "constitutional limitations".[1]

Irenaeus and his pupils had to construct their theory of the Apostolic succession upon a ground which varied greatly according to the different constitutional traditions which prevailed in the provinces of the Church to which they belonged. Rome showed the marks of her earlier constitutional developments by the fact that the title of *episcopus* had not yet been officially introduced for her ecclesiastical leader, but that he was rather called "the president".[2] In Gaul the title of *episcopus* found no opposition, but there the system of Church administration was tending towards a diocesan scheme rather than to one of bishops instituted in every township—quite different, as we have seen, from the African system. Several Churches in that province (Gaul) had only one bishop as their common head. Pothinus, at any rate, had been in charge of Lyons together with Vienne; and it is to be believed that Irenaeus succeeded him in that charge. The arrangement seems to have continued until much later times, if the report of Theodore of Mopsuestia may be accepted as a correct presentation of conditions in Gaul. For this Father mentions that at his time in the West an imperial province (*exarchia*) as such would have two or three bishops, who were in charge of the whole region.[3] In Africa, on the other hand, it was the tradition of the Church that the laity had a considerable

---

[1] Four orders: *Monog.* 11, enumerating them, continues, *quomodo totum ordinem ecclesiae de monogamis disposuit;* cf. also the case of the bishop who made a virgin an honorary widow, because there was no order of virgins, *Virg. vel.* 9. No woman should baptize, *Virg. vel. ib.; Bapt.* 17. 4 ff., cf. *Didasc. Syr.* 3. 9. 1 with Funk's note. Lay baptism and Eucharist, *Exhort. Cast.* 7 *digamus tinguis, digamus offers?* Deserting clergy, *Fuga* 11. *Omnia licet episcopis, Monog.* 12.

[2] There is no evidence available that in any of the other great centres the title of *episcopus* was avoided in official speech. Ignatius of Antioch gives conclusive evidence for the opposite tendency prevailing at his Church.

[3] Diocesan system in Gaul, cf. K. Mueller, *Abh.* Berlin (1922), nr. 3. The same point as Mueller's had been made already by Duchesne, and Harnack's objections, *Mission,* 4th ed., 1. 467, are unconvincing.—Theod. Mopsuest., *Comm.* 1 *Tim.* 3: 8 ed. Swete 2, 124 ff. Swete's note, following Lightfoot, *Philippians* 210 ff., assumes without evident necessity that these two or three bishops resided in the same town.

influence upon the administration even of the divine
service. In principle they were still at liberty to function
as priests in the celebration of the Sacraments, even though
the authority of the clergy was probably altogether beyond
question. This tradition also survived for many centuries,
at any rate in so far as the schismatic Donatist Church was
concerned. Augustine of Hippo still felt it necessary to put
the angry question, "or do you believe you may be saved
without having bishops and clergy, though not without the
Christian religion?"[1] All these different systems of Church
administration would have tended to become sources of
division had it not been for the increase of authority, which
not only the episcopate but indeed the entire ministry of the
Church received through the establishment of the doctrine
of the Apostolic succession of the bishops. Irenaeus, who was
the first to teach this as a doctrine, may therefore be regarded
as the Father who laid the foundations of constitutional
unity within the Western Church. Even so, there was still
need for the gigantic effort of Cyprian of Carthage, who
sought to turn into a living reality that which in the work
of Irenaeus had been, perhaps, little more than a vision of
unity.[2]

[1] Augustine, *Adv. Crescon.* 2. 13.
[2] The influence of Irenaeus upon the theological position taken by Cyprian,
and in particular upon that in his *De Unitate,* would demand a special investigation, which is out of the question here.

# 6

## *The Succession at Alexandria and Origen*

IRENAEUS and his pupils had developed within the
Western Church a form of the doctrine of the Apostolic
succession which was shortly afterwards to receive its
classical form in the writings of Cyprian of Carthage. His
expostulations in *De Unitate* and in several of his letters make
it clear that he did not add anything new to the doctrine,
but only used his unique gift of style to give the convictions
of his time a perfect expression. For this reason it has been
unnecessary to include him in this study, which deals only
with the early stages of the evolution of the doctrine of the
Apostolic succession. It is much more important to turn to
Alexandria, where by the very nature of things the development had been retarded. Alexandria had been in the centre
of that great controversy which during the greater part of
the second century goes by the name of Gnosticism. This
combination of visionary and speculative Christianity—
two attitudes which go very well together—had almost
overwhelmed the Catholic Church in that city. For the time
being, at any rate, the feeling for Church order and the
institutional ministry had been largely submerged, and
when it began to recover, the other Churches—and in
particular Rome—had taken the lead.[1]

The question therefore is whether Alexandria accepted
the Roman system or not. On the whole it can be said that
the East did not refuse to follow the lead from the West in
matters of Church order. 1 Clement had a greater influence
by far over the Eastern Churches than in the West, and
Hippolytus' Apostolic Tradition was destined to play a
similar part. Some doubt as to the conformity of Alexandria

[1] On Cyprian cf. Dom J. Chapman, *Studies on the Early Papacy* (1928) 28 ff.,
who gives a one-sided but useful introduction, and my article *Church Quarterly
Review* (1941–42) 178 ff.

is, however, created by the reports of Jerome and others that before the accession of Heraclas (A.D. 231–46) the bishop of Alexandria had been consecrated by his presbyters. Bishop Gore and Dom F. Cabrol[1] have attempted to disprove this report by showing either that it is erroneous, because Origen did not mention this change so far as we know in his writings, or that, if this argument should not prove conclusive, Jerome could not have referred to the consecration but only to the selection of the bishop by the presbytery. The silence of Origen—or rather his witness—will form the main subject of this chapter. The question of the historical possibility of the consecration of the bishop of Alexandria by his presbytery, however, cannot be wholly answered in that way. For this reason therefore it may be worth while to set out certain observations derived from other sources.

The first observation is the absence of sources which indicate that the bishop of Alexandria was consecrated by way of a ritual which included the laying on of hands. A very feeble support for such a supposition is, perhaps, deducible from a remark of Origen's. He seems to have compared the confirmation of baptism with the ordination of ministers. Addressing laymen he said, "for we all who have been anointed with the unction of the sacred oil are priests".[2] Origen's object in making this statement was to describe confirmation as the ordination of the lay members of the Church. He himself, when making this statement, was a presbyter and, as will be seen, very proud of this distinction. The unction was very closely connected with the laying on of hands in the confirmation ritual of his time; it may be concluded, therefore, that it was also practised at the ordination of presbyters and—possibly—at the ordination of the bishop of Alexandria.

Secondly, if this analogy is accepted, Clement of Alexandria shows that at the confirmation ceremony in Alex-

[1] Consecration of bishops at Alexandria, cf. for the sources B. J. Kidd, *History of the Church to 261 A.D.* 1. 379 ff. Bishop Gore, *J.T.S.* 3 (1902) 278 ff.; *Church and Ministry*, revised by C. H. Turner (1936) 118–26; 315–20. Dom F. Cabrol, *Dict. Arch. Chrét.* 1. 1, 1204 ff., cf. K. D. Mackenzie, *The Case for Episcopacy* (1929) 16 n. 3; 42 ff.; K. Mueller, *Z.N.W.* 28 (1929) 278; 283.
[2] Origen, *Hom. Lev.* 9: 9 *Werke* 6, 436, 9 ff.

andria presbyters performed the laying on of hands. Criticizing fashionable ladies for their wearing of wigs at this service, he said: "Upon whom then shall the presbyter lay hands? whom shall he bless? Not the woman who is thus adorned, but upon somebody else's hair and consequently another head."[1]

Thirdly, it follows from the late *canones Hippolyti* that a presbyter might lay hands upon the bishop of Alexandria at his consecration in the late fourth century. For there the words "and presbyters" were added to the original rule concerning the consecration of bishops contained in Hippolytus' Apostolic Tradition, as follows: "one of the bishops *and presbyters* shall be chosen to lay hands upon him and pray . . .". This was the canon law of Alexandria in the late fourth century, and the alteration is evidence for the strong position of the presbyterate there in the time of Jerome. For these reasons it seems wise to suspend judgment upon the success of Bishop Gore's attack.[2]

The real significance of all this will become evident only when it is seen in its proper context. That context cannot be provided from any earlier Father than Origen. For the evidence derived from Clement of Alexandria, his teacher, is limited and, such as it is, shows little regard for the institutional ministry.[3] Clement in all his writings gave first consideration not to the bishop but to the Catholic gnostic:

> For it is still open to those who devote themselves to the command of the Lord, who live perfect and gnostic lives, according to the Gospel, to be added to the list of the Apostles. Such a man is in fact a presbyter of the Church, and a true deacon of the Divine will, if he acts and teaches the things of the Lord—not chosen by man, neither regarded as just because he is a presbyter, but counted among the

---

[1] Clem. Alex., *Paed.* 3. 63. 1; cf. *Didasc. Lat.* 3. 8. 1, which grants this privilege of laying on of hands even to widows, a clause tacitly abandoned by the Apostolic Constitutions.

[2] *Canones Hippolyti*, Achelis 2. 7–10; Riedel, 2. 201, quoted after K. Mueller, *Z.N.W.* 23 (1924), 227 sq.

[3] The example of St. John, combining the ministries of Apostle and bishop in Clement's *Quis Dives*, is so singular that I hesitate to use it as an example without entering upon the whole Johannine problem, which is obviously impossible here. Moreover, it does not belong to Alexandria but to Asia Minor (Ephesus).

presbyterate because he is just. If such a man is not preferred to the *protocathedria* here on earth, he will be placed upon one of the twenty-four thrones to judge the people, as St. John says in the Revelation. (*Strom.* 6. 106. 1.)

Such a gnostic was, according to Clement, the true spiritual authority within the Church; and the *protocathedria* which by right belonged to him was a comparatively unimportant perquisite which the gnostic, although he was entitled to it, could easily forgo. Elsewhere, Clement maintained that the presbyterate, which existed within the earthly Church, was the image of the heavenly ministry. Episcopacy was not yet clearly distinguished by Clement from the presbyterate.[1]

Under Pantaenus and Clement the catechetical school had been the backbone of Catholic doctrine at Alexandria, where the case for Catholicism had been stated in opposition to the numerous kinds of Gnosticism. Traditions about these two teachers were still alive at the time of Eusebius. On the other hand, the names of the bishops in the list from Africanus, which Eusebius embodied in his canon, are no more than names. That suggests strongly that the catechetical school at Alexandria was not a place which supported the bishops' authority without question. It is indicative of the slow growth of the episcopate's strength that Demetrius, who was the virtual founder of the Patriarchate at Alexandria (A.D. 189–231), at first had to condone the eccentricity of Origen, the young head of the school, and only after his departure from Alexandria made known his disapproval. It is to be assumed that Origen's departure was connected with the growing authority of Demetrius as bishop of the Church. The successor of Demetrius, Heraclas, who had previously been the pupil and the successor of Origen in the headship of the catechetical school, was forced by the very nature of things, despite his earlier close connexion with Origen, to continue the struggle. For it was

---

[1] Clem. Alex., *Strom.* 7. 3. 3. The index of O. Staehlin to *Clement Werke* 4. 669, s.v. *presbyteros*, makes it clear how small a part was played by the institutional ministry in Cl.'s theology.—Episcopacy, cf. K. Mueller, *Z.N.W.* 28 (1929), 288. It is difficult to see why K. D. Mackenzie, *The Case for Episcopacy* 43 n. 1, should copy Bishop Gore's reference to Clement's casual remark *Paed.* 3. 97. 2, for the only remarkable feature is that the presbytery is mentioned first, receiving preference over the bishop.

necessary to decide what should be the future relationship
between Christian scholarship and Church authority.[1]

In view of the fact that Origen was forced to hold a party
position it is not surprising that he should in his writings
reflect upon rather than actively participate in the evolution
of the doctrine of the Apostolic succession at Alexandria. A
certain—genuine or fictitious—disinterestedness in constitutional matters was well suited to the prevailing circumstances. Thus the silence of Origen regarding any change
of the consecration rite at the accession of Heraclas, even if
such a change were attested elsewhere, as well as his silence
about the differences between the Alexandrian rite and
usages elsewhere, would not be particularly surprising.[2] Perhaps it is an overstatement that "Origen knew nothing of a
special *charisma* of the episcopacy", but it is at least remarkable that references to the bishops are absent from a passage
in Origen's commentary on Romans where he discusses the
special *charisma* of the Apostles and refers to their "equals".
The context makes it clear that these were on the one hand
the "prophets and teachers" and, on the other, the whole
Catholic Church. The importance of the institutional
ministry is diminished also because, as K. Mueller has
rightly observed, in Origen's theology "the earthly and the
heavenly Church, the visible sanctuary and that within
man's soul, are constantly intermingled."[3] Like Clement of
Alexandria, Origen regarded the Saints, "ecclesiastical
men instructed by the divine wisdom", as being nearest to
the divine truth. From the manner in which in this context
he dealt with men like Marcion and "Ebion", it appears
that he regarded their endeavours as comparable with the
achievements of St. Paul, although he admits that faults
and weaknesses for which they themselves had been re-

[1] On Demetrius and Origen cf. Euseb., *H.E.* 6. 8. 3 ff., unjustly laying all the
blame on Demetrius. On Heraclas and Origen cf. K. Mueller-v. Campenhausen,
*Kirchen-Gesch.* 1. 1, 3rd ed., 303, and Euseb., *H.E.* 6. 3. 2.

[2] The *argumentum e silentio* of Origen, not a very conclusive one in any case,
has been put most feebly by K. D. Mackenzie, *op. cit.* 43.

[3] K. Mueller, *Z.N.W.* 28 (1929), 287.—Origen, *Comm. Rom.* 7. 5 Lo. 7.
108 ff., which makes it improbable that the "priests equal to the Apostles",
*Orat.* 28. 9, should be the bishops. Cf. also, how Origen, *ad Mart.* 30 fin.
*Werke* 1. 30. 5 ff., describes the martyrs as priests under the High Priest Jesus
Christ, like Him at the same time priest and sacrifice.

sponsible had led them astray. Such "ecclesiastical men" therefore had the first claim to be equated with the Apostles, and not those whose ambition was satisfied in the earthly Church with a bishopric.[1]

It is noticeable that in those places where Origen made direct reference to the Apostolic succession it was hardly ever to the succession of bishops. Only when he described Ignatius as the saint who had been the second bishop of Antioch after St. Peter is the episcopal succession plainly stated. This was an *obiter dictum*, but for us it is valuable in that it shows clearly that Origen did not regard St. Peter as the first bishop of Antioch. That position had been held by Euodius.[2] So far, therefore, Origen conformed to the views of other contemporary compilers of succession lists, such as Hegesippus or Irenaeus. There is also one other remark in which Origen referred to the Apostolic succession of bishops —that is, in his allegorical interpretation of the parable of the good Samaritan:

> the innkeeper represents the Apostles and their successors, bishops, and teachers of the Church—or those angels who are in charge of the defence of the Church.

This allegorical exegesis rested upon a firm tradition. One of the chief duties of a bishop, from the earliest days of the Church, had been to show hospitality; and to that extent we suggest that Origen was adopting an earlier interpretation. No such support, however, can be found for the place of the Apostles and teachers in the interpretation, and this, together with most of the other allegories, seems to have been his own contribution. It is significant of this personal touch that the Latin version of Origen's commentary on St. Luke abandoned the whole interpretation and said, "the innkeeper is beyond doubt the protecting angel of the Church." The words "beyond doubt" have a strongly polemical ring. Origen's general tendency, which was to

---

[1] Saints and ecclesiastical men, *Comm. Rom.* 3: 1; 11 Lo. 6, 170; 228.—Marcion and Ebion, *Comm. Rom.* 3: 11 cit.—Ambition, *Comm. Rom.* 2: 2 Lo. 6, 72.

[2] *Hom. Luk.* 6 *Werke* 9. 37. 4 ff. W. Bauer, *Rechtglaeubigkeit* (1934) 120, is mistaken in assuming that St. Peter was regarded as the first bishop of Antioch by Origen and in Euseb., *H.E.* 3. 36. 2. This place is expressly ascribed to Euodius in Euseb., *H.E.* 3. 22 and in his Canon. Bauer seems to have been misled by his anti-Roman prejudice.

regard the whole Church as in the succession, *diadoche*, of the teaching of Jesus, did not find much favour with the later Western Church and it seems to have been rejected together with his reference to teachers, Apostles, and bishops, and the whole remark about the Apostolic succession.[1]

This apparent intolerance on the part of the Western Church becomes more understandable when it is seen how Origen in his other remarks on the Apostolic succession failed to mention the bishops at all. The one from his *De Principiis* has been marked out by Harnack, who, however, has not said a word about this significant omission of the bishops:

> The rule and discipline which the Apostles have received from Jesus Christ, and which they have handed on *per successionem* to those after them who are teachers within the Holy Church.

This sentence shows clearly that Origen in his youth saw his own task of teacher as being in direct relation to the Apostolic tradition and succession.[2] Drawn quite independently, his conclusion was yet similar to that of Irenaeus, who had stated that the Apostolic tradition and succession belonged together. Irenaeus, however, had combined in his own person the two qualities of teacher and bishop, and therefore had found no difficulty in vesting the succession of teachers in the episcopal succession. Origen, the last independent teacher at Alexandria, was less well placed; for in his conception of teacher there was only imperfectly concealed the earlier conception of Christian gnostic which underlay it. It is also clearly discernible in the wording of the same passage in the *Philocalia*, that anthology from the works of Origen collected by Gregory of Nyssa and Basil the Great: "to those who are endowed with the standard of the heavenly Church of Jesus Christ, according to the succession of the Apostles."[3] Rufinus in his Latin version, on

[1] Good Samaritan, *Hom. Luk.* 34 *Werke* 9. 202. Latin, *ib.* p. 204, 22 ff., cf. also *Comm. Rom.* 9. 31 Lo. 7. 336 ff. *Diadoche, Philocalia* ed. Armitage-Robinson (1893) 88, 29.

[2] Origen, *Princ.* 4. 9, quoted after Harnack, *Mission*, 4th ed., 1. 360 ff. This sentence is remarkable in that it forms an exception to the general rule stated by C. H. Turner, *Studies* (1912) 25, that the teachers to whom Origen referred were presbyters.

[3] *Philocalia* 1. 9 ed. Armitage-Robinson 16. 4 ff.

the other hand, seems to have seen every teacher of the Church in this succession. External as well as internal evidence makes it probable that Gregory and Basil were nearer the original. This is shown especially by the last passage, which makes direct reference to the Apostolic succession, in Origen's *De Oratione:*[1]

> For thus both, the Apostles themselves and those who are regarded as their equals, being priests under the great High Priest and having received understanding in respect of Divine worship, know by the instruction of the Divine Spirit . . . .

This remark points clearly to a succession of gnostics in the Holy Spirit. For the priesthood of the Apostles is, as has been seen, a heavenly priesthood. Origen in this work, which is also an early one, clearly followed Clement of Alexandria, and assumed that the true priesthood of the Christian gnostic made him equal to the Apostles and thus removed the distinction between the heavenly and the earthly Church.[2]

To Origen the heavenly and the earthly Church were so closely related that the question of the Apostolic succession lost some of its urgency. He could describe how an ardent Christian arrived at an entirely pagan town, gathered a congregation around him, converted them, baptized them, and eventually became their bishop; but in reality he maintained that the angel guarding this Church had founded, protected, and guided it, until it had been finally established.[3] The unity of the angelic Church guaranteed the continuity and coherence of the earthly Church in such cases. Neither was this theory Origen's property alone, for it had already been held by Clement of Alexandria whose belief it was, as we have seen, that presbyters and deacons in the earthly Church only reflected the ministrations of the angels. It seems, however, that Origen, claiming that every Church had actually two bishops, one angelic and the other human, advanced beyond Clement's theory. In so doing he was conscious of the fact that his theory was in reality an adaptation of the pagan doctrine that each nation had its national

---

[1] *De Orat.* 28. 9, cf. *Comm. Rom.* 7. 5. Lo. 7, 108 ff.

[2] Clem. Alex., *Strom.* 6. 106. 1.

[3] *Hom. Num.* 11. 4 *Werke* 7. 84. 16, cf. Harnack *T.U.* 42 .3 (1919) 75 n. 4, and *Hom. Luk.* 13 *Werke* 9. 91. 20 ff.

angel, a doctrine found also in Jewish apocryphal writings but neither in the Old nor in the New Testament.[1] These protecting angels were charged above all with the worship that was offered up in their several Churches. Accordingly, as the ministry of the Word was not granted exclusively, or even mainly, to the bishops by Origen, the succession of bishops suffered degradation. For the message of the Apostles was directed to him who was *dux et doctor* of his Church, the gnostic, who might or might not be the bishop, warning him of pride and conceit, and enjoining upon him the humility of Apostolic conduct.[2]

As Origen emphasized the succession of gnostic teachers, which was derived not so much from an unbroken chain of predecessors as from a living contact with the Church of the Holy Spirit, he was led to a high appreciation of the living faith resident in the individual Christian. This attitude found its expression above all in his pamphlet addressed to the martyrs. Jesus Christ, so he said, by sacrificing His own life to the Father, had become the great High Priest of God, through whom all offerings to the Father had to be made. It followed, therefore, that the martyrs, who also offered their lives to the Father, in so doing acquired the dignity of priests. The sentiment upon which this view was founded was fairly general at the time of Origen and found its expression also in the Apostolic Tradition of Hippolytus, which ruled that a martyr who had been in chains was a presbyter without ordination (*cheirotonein*). Origen, however, wished to emphasize that the crowned martyrs would be endowed with the priesthood in the heavenly Church. Neither was he above expanding and sentimentalizing this promise. For he used it in an attack upon those "objectionable High Priests" who ventured to say that they led saintlier lives than the simple martyrs, ascetics, or virgins. Did not

---

[1] Clem. Alex., *Strom.* 7. 3. 1–4, cf. K. Mueller, *Z.N.W.* 28 (1929), 288. Two bishops, *Hom. Luk.* 13 cit. On the guardianship of the ministering spirits over the infant Church cf. *Comm. Rom.* 7. 5 Lo. 7, 105 ff. National angels; cf. also *adv. Cels.* 8. 33 fin.; *Comm. Matt.* 14. 13 *Werke* 10. 309. 32 ff.; *Comm. Rom.* 8. 11 Lo. 7. 266 ff. The same idea occurs in Hippol., *Comm. Dan.* 3. 9. 10 *Werke* 1. 1. 142. 4 ff.; Ps. Clem., *Hom.* 18. 4 Lag. 170. 8 ff. Pagan, cf. F. Cumont, *Oriental. Religionen* (German translation by Burckhardt-Brandenberg), 3rd ed. (1931), 140.

[2] *Dux et doctor*, *Comm. Rom.* 2: 11 Lo. 6. 114 ff.

these simple souls, "having entrusted themselves unto God and accepting the teaching of Jesus, put away lusts and uncleanness and unseemly behaviour, so that, after the manner of initiated priests, many of them repudiated all intercourse and remained wholly undefiled"?[1]

Here were opinions which differed characteristically from the Roman view, and the same may be said about Origen's theory, in which he agreed with Tertullian, that because of their potential priesthood all Christians should practise continence, at least in so far as to be satisfied with monogamy—a rule which under his influence seems to have made its way even into the *Apostolic Constitutions*. It is also evident that he found a close kinship between the ascetics and virgins on the one hand and the Church of the angels on the other.[2] Still more pronounced was his advocacy of individual piety. His ultimate conviction was that martyr-dom and asceticism were no more than the outward signs of the Church within man's soul. Ideas of macro- and microcosm, originating from Stoic and Neo-Platonic sources, were combined in Origen's allegorical exegesis of the tabernacle in his *Homilies on Exodus*, which for us are the main source of information about these conceptions. The same subject was resumed in various remarks on Leviticus and even in his book against Celsus. In all these passages Origen stressed the priestly character of man's own self, worshipping God within the tabernacle of the soul:

> For this one you may hold for certain, that, although you may be neglected and ignored by men, you nevertheless perform before God the obligations of the priesthood within the temple of your soul.[3]

---

[1] Jesus the High Priest, *Comm. Rom.* 1: 9 Lo. 6, 34, cf. *Didasc. Syr.* 2. 26. 1 *principi sacerdotum Christo et ministris eius.* On the imitation of Christ's sufferings by the martyrs cf. E. Lucius-Anrich, *Anfaenge des Heiligenkults* (1904) 52 ff., who have even overlooked passages like Hippol., *Comm. Dan.* 1. 17. 8 *Werke* 1. 1. 28 ff., "the martyrs saved through the blood of Christ"; Tert., *Pud.* 22, *si propterea Christus in martyre est; Didasc. Syr.* 5. 3. 3. Martyrs are automatically presbyters, Hippol., *Ap. Trad.* 10. 1. Heavenly priesthood, Origen, *ad Mart.* 30 *Werke* 1, 29 ff.; cf. *Comm. Rom.* 7: 3 Lo. 7. 92–95, on the relation between the suffering of Christ and that of His martyrs. Wicked priests, *Comm. Matt.* 16: 25 *Werke* 10. 558. 19 ff. Ascetics (quotation) *adv. Cels.* 7. 48.

[2] Monogamy, *Comm. Matt.* 14: 22 *Werke* 10. 336. 20 ff.; *Const. Ap.* 3. 2. 2, cf. Harnack, *T.U.* 42. 4 (1919)., 121 n. 1. Ascetics and angels, *Comm. Matt.* 15: 25 *Werke* 10. 424. 19 ff.

[3] Tabernacle within man's soul, *Hom. Exod.* 9: 4 *Werke* 6. 240. 22 ff.; 241. 18 ff.; 242. 22 ff.; 243. 22 ff.; *Hom. Lev.* 2: 4; 9: 9 *Werke* 6. 294. 30 ff.; 436. 9 ff.; *adv. Cels.* 8. 74. Quotation., *Hom. Lev.* 6: 5 *Werke* 6. 367. 9 ff.

This conviction lent itself equally to a friendly or to a hostile attitude towards the institutional ministry within the earthly Church. This alternative found its expression in a remark in Origen's commentary on the Song of Songs which at first sight may not appear to have any special significance:[1]

> How should we not show towards the Saints who have been our Fathers in Christ, and also the pastors and bishops and the presbyters who are charged with the ministry of the Word, when they serve well in the Church and excel in faith before the others, an affection of far greater tenderness for their manifold merits, than that which may arise in respect of those who have only performed part of these duties—or nothing at all.

This remark shows that the relationship between the Christian minister and his people was regarded as being largely personal and individual. The ministry as such did not, so it seems, endow the clergy with any great claims to a reverent treatment; and a similar reserve apparently obtained among some of Origen's followers also, a reserve which was extended to the authority claimed by the clergy in matters of Christian doctrine:[2]

> If any doubt should arise which cannot be settled by us, Jesus should be unanimously approached, who is always present where two or three are gathered together in His Name. . . . Neither is it absurd to ask one of the teachers instituted by God in the Church, for a solution.

The chief source of illumination, according to this recommendation of Origen's, was the private prayer-meeting. The teaching ministry of the Church was represented as a possible alternative; but from the slightly supercilious "neither is it absurd" it may be deduced that Origen was addressing an enthusiastic audience which preferred to put its trust rather in prophetic enlightenments than in a commonplace performance of the duties of the institutional ministry.

The individual character of Origen's approach to the doctrine of the Apostolic succession is obvious. It was in many respects that of the Catholic gnostic, and in so far as it was dependent upon earlier views it was that of the head of the catechetical school at Alexandria. It was influenced by pagan philosophical speculations. This was only to be

---

[1] Origen, *Comm. Cant.* 3 *Werke* 8. 189. 6 ff.
[2] *Comm. Matt.* 13: 15 *Werke* 10. 216. 25 ff.

expected and it was not denied by Origen either, who held
that Abraham and Abimelech, the religion of Israel and
the wisdom of the Gentiles, had been combined at the hands
of Christ.[1] From these high ideals Origen was compelled to
look down upon the realities of Church life and administration, and these filled him with dismay. Various scan-
dalous stories about bishops were rumoured at that time,
of which Hippolytus' report on the career of Pope Callistus
may be mentioned as their prototype, because this author
has given to his readers the complete facts, so far as he
believed them to be true. This method was not the usual
way, which generally consisted of hints regarding one
bishop or another—more or less vague allusions to behaviour unbecoming a Christian bishop. The remark of
Tertullian concerning the Catholic bishop of Uthina in
Africa is one such example; and it is evident from the careful
and cautious report of Eusebius that a whole library of
gossip might have been filled with stories about bishop
Narcissus and his adversaries at Jerusalem. Origen is
representative of the reasoned criticism of a man whose
mind was troubled by the obvious dangers into which the
Church was plunging because of the inevitable increase in
the status of the clergy, as a result of the emphasis laid upon
the Apostolic succession of the bishops. This emphasis gave
rise to the impression that the clergy were the basis of Church
organization. Origen indicates the general nature of abuses
to be found both in the appointment as well as in the conduct of Christian ministers. It has to be realized, however,
that these statements, some of which contain very cutting
remarks, were made in the course of his controversy with
the Alexandrian Patriarchate. They were pleadings of his
special case and should be read as such.[2]

[1] Abimelech, *Comm. Gen.* 6: 2 *Werke* 6. 67. 28 ff., cf. *ib.* 14. 3 p. 123, *moralis vero et physica quae dicitur philosophia paene omnis quae nostra sunt, sentit.*

[2] Tert. *Monog.* 12 *omnia licet episcopo, sicut ille vester Uthinensis nec Scantiniam timuit,* referring to a *lex Scantinia de nefanda Venere,* cf. Cic. *ad Fam.* 8. 12. 3; 14. 4; *Phil.* 3. 6; Juvenal 2. 44; Auson., *Epigr.* 92. 4 (Peiper).—Narcissus, Euseb., *H.E.,* 6. 8 ff.—In *T.U.* 42. 4 (1919), 117 ff.; 138 ff., Harnack has made a collection of Origen's indictments of the ministry, which, however, is incomplete and gives no indication as to its relation to general Church history. —Origen's views seem to have been summarized by Aphraates the Persian Sage, *Hom.* 10. 5, German version by Bert, *T.U.* 3. 3/4 (1888), 162.

The most serious initial mistake against which Origen felt it necessary to warn his audience was that of desiring a bishopric for external reasons. Having castigated vain and selfish preachers, Origen continued:[1]

> The same has to be said of a person who hankers after a bishopric, because of its glory amongst men or because of the presents made by those, who are attending at his sermon, as a sign of reverence.

This attack was delivered without any provocation in the course of an exegesis of Matthew 15: 22. Origen himself eventually became aware of this, for after having carried the attack still further, he justified himself to his hearers, "if these remarks seem to be out of the way, look around and say, whether they are also unnecessary". It seems reasonable therefore to suggest that this kind of attack belonged to Origen's stock in trade and very probably to that of the catechetical school at Alexandria under his headship. This submission seems to follow from the way in which he turned the saying of Clement of Alexandria about the priesthood of every gnostic into a weapon against the institutional ministry:

> Therefore what profit shall I have occupying the first place in splendour, receiving the honour due to the great and still not satisfied, that what I have is equal to my dignity? Shall I not be punished more severely for having been honoured as just by all, whereas in matter of fact I have been a sinner?

This saying was preceded somewhat earlier by the definite statement that "he who is the bishop of a church and does wrong, will have the greater punishment". For this reason Origen also gave his audience the advice, "that it is good for a man not to rush into dignities, prelacies, and ministries of the Church, for they all come from God."[2]

Those ambitious men who acted contrary to this advice would be at the same time ignorant and conceited, for "frequently the reason for the conceit of the ignorant is that he possesses the dignity of the priesthood or the diaconate."[3] Further, such ministers would almost inevitably be led by their conceitedness to imitate the officers of the

---

[1] Origen, *Comm. Matt.* 11: 15 *Werke* 10. 59. 17 ff.

[2] Apology, Origen, *ib.* Greater punishment, taken from a longer passage in *Hom. Ez.* 5: 4 *Werke* 8. 375. 2 ff. Not rush, *Hom. Is.* 6: 1 *Werke* 8. 269. 9 ff. All these remarks are, of course, dependent upon Jas. 3: 1.

[3] Origen, *Hom. Ez.* 9: 2 *Werke* 8. 409. 10 ff.

secular powers, a thing to be avoided by the bishops, "for he who is called is not called to be a prince, but the servant of the entire congregation; and if you will believe Holy Scripture, take the advice of our Lord and Saviour, that he who wants to be first in the Church let him be the servant of all (Matthew 20: 26 ff.). Therefore, the prince of the Church is bound to be a slave, that he may rise from the servitude to the heavenly tribunal, as it is written, 'ye shall sit upon twelve thrones to judge the tribes of Israel' (Matthew 19: 28)." Here again we come upon a "rehash" of Clement's statement about the gnostic, made for the purpose of contrasting the ideal ministry with a very unsatisfactory reality.[1] For in actual practice many ministers were slovenly and selfish, "called a pastor, but not chosen a pastor, such a one who, being at the head of his flock, uses its milk and dresses in its wool, but does not visit the infirm, neither carries the lame, but overburdens the strong with labour." There were frequent cases of fraud and corruption to be found among the clergy, who would "convert to their own benefit the offerings made to God and the endowments of the poor fund".[2]

For all these gross negligences the punishment would be severe:

> For you must know that the priesthood gives no guarantee of salvation. For many a priest will go unto perdition and many laymen will be received into blessedness. . . . For what is helpful is not a seat among the presbyterate, but a life worthy of that vocation.

People should therefore understand what a great risk was entailed in ordination to the ministry:

> For more is demanded of me [the presbyter] than of a deacon, and more of a deacon than of a layman, and he who has been entrusted with the ecclesiastical authority over all of us, still more will be demanded of him.[3]

---

[1] Imitation of secular officials, *Comm. Matt.* 16: 8 *Werke* 10. 294. 32 ff. Servant of all, *Hom. Is.* 6: 1 *Werke* 8. 269. 18 ff. Here as well as in the preceding paragraph the parallel from Clement is always *Strom.* 6. 106. 1 ff.

[2] Called but not chosen, *Comm. Rom.* 1: 2 Lo. 6. 16. Fraud, *ib.* 2: 11 Lo. 6. 115. Such derelictions of duty were facilitated by the prevailing lack of control. For the entire distribution of alms was centralized in the bishop, Justin 1. *Apol.* 67. 7; *Didasc. Syr.* 2. 27. 1; 28. 7. Another but less characteristic attack of the same kind may be found in *Comm. Rom.* 9: 3 Lo. 7. 309 ff., and one upon the lower orders of the clergy, presbyters and deacons, *ib.* 8: 9 Lo. 7. 253 ff.

[3] The two quotations are from *Hom. Ez.* 9: 2 *Werke* 3. 80. 15–81, 10.

Consequently, warnings were repeatedly given to Christian
ministers by Origen, who referred in particular to Romans
2: 3, for St. Paul had not had pagan rulers in his mind
when he had written this solemn caution, but the princes
and leaders of the Churches, the bishops, presbyters, and
deacons, that "they should not believe that they would
escape the judgment of God".[1] The Bible made it clear
that although a man had been called to be an Apostle or
another appointed as a prophet, yet he because of his
negligence and disobedience could forfeit his vocation,
like Judas Iscariot or the unknown prophet who had been
sent to Jeroboam the king.[2] A dark picture indeed was thus
drawn by Origen, but it cannot be denied that its features
may be confirmed from several other sources. We are
frequently met by statements to the effect that the dis-
appointment of ambitious but unsuccessful competitors for a
bishopric was among the main causes for most heresies and
schisms; and warnings against clerical careerism and
ambition are to be found not only in the Shepherd of
Hermas,[3] but still earlier in the Gospel, when the mother of
the sons of Zebedee came to ask of the Lord "a certain
thing" (Matt. 20: 20). The imitation of pagan officials,
forbidden by the Lord in the same chapter (vv. 25–26), was
used by Tertullian for his angry denunciation of Pope
Callistus who had issued a peremptory edict after the manner
of the pagan High Pontiff. The same complaint of having
imitated the manners of pagan high officials was made in
the indictment of Paul of Samosata at the second (third?)
synod held against him at Antioch; and for the various
other accusations regarding the corruption of the clergy
reference may be made to Harnack.[4] Of a more general
interest is the fact shown by an apocryphal text—written
probably in Egypt before the end of the second century—

[1] Rom. 2: 3, cf. e.g. *Comm. Rom.* 2: 2 Lo. 6, 71 ff.
[2] Apostle and prophet, *Comm. Rom.* 1: 2. Lo. 6, 15.
[3] Herm., *Mand.* 11. 12, cf. *Vis.* 2. 2. 6. The most notable names of men who
turned heretics, because they had been unsuccessful in the bid for a bishopric,
are Valentinus of Rome, Tert., *adv. Val.* 4, and Theboutis of Jerusalem, Euseb.,
*H.E.* 4. 22. 5.
[4] Pope Callistus, Tert. *Pud.* 1.—Paul of Samosata, Euseb., *H.E.* 7. 30. —
Harnack, *T.U.* 42. 4, 118 ff., cf. *Mission*, 4th ed., 1. 234, with special reference
to the cases contained in Cyprian's correspondence.

that the severe punishment of disloyal clergy was already a subject of popular discussion:

> And there will come a punishment upon the bishops and *pastophoroi* for seducing my people for the satisfaction of their lusts.[1]

The reason why these accusations against bishops and clergy have been recorded here is not that reflections may be cast upon either side of the conflict, but because it forms part of that background which has to be provided for the most circumstantial, the most elaborate and, in many respects, the most serious of all Origen's attacks. For by studying his violent indictment of the graft which prevailed in so many cases at the appointment of bishops and other clergy, we find that Origen has given us valuable hints of the procedure as well as of the doctrine concerning the appointment of bishops and other ministers. First of all, in one of his homilies on Joshua,[2] he outlined the final model for the appointment of bishops:

> When it was necessary to substitute another man in the place of Judas, the Apostles forgathered, who in any case were much wiser than those who nowadays ordain bishops, presbyters, and deacons, and selected two and placed them in their midst; neither did they allow themselves any preference as to who should be appointed, but they prayed and cast lots etc.

This, unfortunately, was no longer the practice, much rather was it the case that would-be candidates used "simony"—not yet called by this name—i.e. bribery and canvassing of the multitude—to obtain the popular vote. The authorities in charge, on the other hand, limited their selection in frequent cases to the members of certain privileged, one might almost say priestly, families. It is therefore of great significance that Origen confronted this practice with that governing the appointment of Joshua as the successor of Moses, at which *nulla consanguinitatis ratio* had been taken into account.[3] For the appointment of Joshua had for long been regarded as the model for the appointment of the Rabbis in the Jewish Synagogue.

[1] *Epist. Apost.* 9 ed. C. Schmidt-Wajnberg (*T.U.* 43, 1919) 64*.
[2] Origen, *Hom. Jos.* 23: 2 *Werke* 7. 441. 3 ff.
[3] Origen, *Hom. Num.* 22: 4 *Werke* 7. 208. 24 ff.

It is instructive, too, to compare these criticisms with
some purely factual reports which, although they may put
a very different complexion upon these matters, do nevertheless show that Origen was not fighting windmills. The
first is the report of Cyprian's biographer, Pontius, about
the election of his hero to the see of Carthage. We hear that
Cyprian at his baptism had given half his fortune to the
Church at Carthage, and that at the next vacancy he was
elected bishop on the strength of the popular vote against
the resistance of a considerable portion of the clergy.
Further, there are two reports about elections from priestly
families. The one is the naïve statement of Polycrates of
Ephesus claiming spiritual authority because "seven of my
relatives have been bishops, and I am the eighth". The other
is the somewhat more sinister-looking declaration of the
second (third?) synod of Antioch, that in the place of the
deposed Paul of Samosata they had appointed to the see
Domnus, whose father had been bishop of the city in times
past.[1]

These preliminary skirmishes found their climax in a
violent and comprehensive attack by Origen, who made
the interpretation of the cleansing of the temple on Palm
Sunday the occasion on which to deliver it. He explained
with great detail that the allegorical significance of the
vendors of doves whose seats were overthrown by the Lord
(Matt. 21: 12) was "those who hand over the churches to
greedy, tyrannical, and wicked bishops or presbyters".
Origen made it equally plain who the people were upon
whom he delivered this attack. They were those who,
"seated boastfully on the seat of Moses, sell entire churches
of doves to such leaders as those referred to in the words of the
Lord in Jeremiah (4: 22, LXX) and Micah (3: 9)." The
allusion in this passage to Matthew 23: 2: "the scribes and
Pharisees sit in Moses' seat", was intentional; it was not made
in the somewhat facile way in which it often appears as a pro-
verb in modern speech. Origen, as we have seen, had referred

[1] Cyprian, cf. *Church Quarterly Review* (1941–42) 185 ff.—Polycrates, Euseb.,
*H.E.* 5. 24. 6.—Domnus, *ib.* 7. 30. 17. The origin of this nepotism may have
been the rise of the Churches from the primitive house-churches; but the later
history of the Church has unfortunately offered many instances of this abuse
even after the abolition of that early institution of house-churches.

to the succession of Joshua after Moses, when denouncing the preference given to members of "priestly" families chosen as candidates for an episcopal see. He did the same again in this context and followed up his remark by an entirely unambiguous description of these successors of Moses who were responsible for the frequent selection of unsuitable persons for the office of clergy:

> Those who have been entrusted with presiding over congregations, the bishops and presbyters who, on the one hand, sell entire churches to unsuitable persons, and on the other ordain undesirable men to the ministry, they are the vendors of doves, and their seats have been overthrown by Jesus.[1]

It has been pointed out already that the succession of Joshua after Moses was the prototype of the Rabbinic succession (with Moses laying hands upon Joshua, Num. 27: 18 ff.; Deut. 34: 9). It has also been shown how in the pseudo-Clementines the seat of Moses, the seat of Jesus, and the seat of St. Peter had been seen as one. The details of the election of Matthias which provide a model for the appointment of bishops, the references to the seat of Moses and to the ordination of Joshua, provide us with a solid body of evidence for the existence of the doctrine of the Apostolic succession of bishops—and possibly other clergy—in Alexandria, founded upon Jewish-Christian beliefs. What we should like to know is how far these views were those of the Patriarchate of Alexandria, to what extent they were used by Origen for argument's sake, and how far they were his own. The answer is not easy. For it is quite clear, on the one hand, that some of Origen's favourite ideas, such as that of the priesthood of man's own self within the sanctuary of his soul, had no Jewish antecedents—barring Philo. It is also evident that Origen took a special delight in explaining that St. Paul had been right, when in Romans 7: 6 he had compared the law of Moses with a dead husband. For, so he said, it was not only in abeyance, but by the destruction of the temple it was truly dead: so much so that,

[1] Origen, *Comm. Matt.* 16: 22 *Werke* 10. 549. 22 ff. The passage has been discussed, somewhat perfunctorily, by Harnack, *T.U.* 42. 4 (1919), 136, who seems to have noticed no more than its obvious moral implications. It is, however, one of the most valuable statements we possess on the ministry and the Church constitution at Alexandria.

as in the rules governing leprosy, the rules themselves had become completely unintelligible to the Jews, and all their sacrificial rites had had to be abolished.[1] It seems difficult not to hear in this exposé the echoes of the traditional Alexandrian hatred for the Jews. Nevertheless, Jewish-Christian teaching was so strong that it forced Origen to use the Jewish term of *archontes* for the clergy, although he protested against the obvious implication that the clergy were a "ruling class" within the Church. For these reasons it seems likely that Origen adopted the Jewish-Christian theory of the Apostolic succession under an influence from outside.[2]

On the other hand, it is also noticeable that Origen most readily derived the priesthood of the Christian clergy from the Old Testament. He even contributed to the theory the observation that the Apostles had combined the rulership with the priesthood, Joshua with Eleazar.[3] He maintained that the chief element of the priesthood was what he regarded as his very own vocation, the ministry of the Word: "the priest being the secret and mystical word of God". It was this same Eleazar who had been first granted the title of *episcopus*, bishop, in Holy Scripture.[4] In this connexion it is significant how when referring to one of the necessary qualities of a bishop, *non percussorem*, 1 Timothy 3: 3, Origen used the term of *doctor ecclesiae*.[5] Being endowed with the priesthood, the bishop had above all his share in the teaching ministry of the Church. In this way the bishops had to be at the service of all their people. Therefore it had been ordained by God that when Joshua was inaugurated as the

---

[1] Origen, *Comm. Rom.* 6: 7 Lo. 7. 34 ff.

[2] *Archontes*, Origen, *Comm. Matt.* 11: 9 *Werke* 10. 49. 13 ff.; cf. above p. 73 f. and E. Friedberg, *Kirchenrecht*, 4th ed., 12 n. 20, who emphasizes that in the Greek the elders of the Synagogue were almost invariably called "the rulers", *archontes*. In pagan sources *archontes* is used mainly for political rulers. The presiding deities of the spheres are also called *archontes*, but I have searched in vain for the use of the word as a description of the heads of a worshipping community.

[3] Origen, *Hom. Jos.* 18: 1 *Werke* 7. 406. 12 ff.

[4] Origen, *Hom. 1, Sam.* 1: 7 *Werke* 8. 12. 22 ff., referring to Num. 4: 16 (LXX).

[5] Origen, *Hom. Exod.* 10: 4 *Werke* 6. 251. 25 ff. It is, of course, true that Origen put a special emphasis upon the duty of preaching to the people because of his close connexion with the catechetical school at Alexandria; but the appointment of Heraclas to the see of Alexandria shows that he was supported in this by the whole Egyptian Church.

successor of Moses the whole congregation of Israel had to
be present. Although Joshua had been chosen by God, the
attendance of the people was still required. This rule also
obtained at the ordination of priests within the Church,
"that they all should know for certain, that the outstanding
person, the most learned, most holy, most prominent in
every virtue, had been chosen to the priesthood, so that no
excuse should be left, no scruple remain." In founding this
view upon 1 Timothy 3: 7, "that he must have a good
report from them who are without", Origen quite uninten-
tionally threw light upon the segregation of the clergy from
the laity which had already taken place by this time, for
"they who are without" were the laity in this context, and
no longer the heathen as in the days of St. Paul.[1]

Origen showed also a remarkable originality when he
based his criticism of the Christian ministry upon Old
Testament and Jewish precedents. He maintained, for
instance, that at his time both the priests called Phinehas
who are mentioned in the Old Testament were to be found
among the clergy: the fiery, dutiful son of Eleazar as well
as the nefarious son of Eli.[2] Such subtlety, which was
characteristic of Origen's exegesis, was probably less common
amongst his opponents. It seems therefore that Origen,
although he may have been compelled to accept this basis,
nevertheless took up the challenge willingly; and although
he tried to be fair to Phinehas, the son of Eleazar, and to
his followers, yet he was on the other hand quite ready to
listen to the complaints, "Look, what a bishop, what a
presbyter, what a deacon . . . when a priest or another
minister of God were seen to infringe their orders and to do
something contrary to the sacerdotal or Levitical order."[3]
It happened far too often that "he who has a mean mind
and cares for the things of this world occupies the exalted

[1] Popular vote, *Hom. Lev.* 6: 3 *Werke* 6. 362. 23 ff.—Those outside, *ib.*, but
cf. *adv. Cels.* 8. 75, where "those outside" is used for the Gentiles.
[2] The two Phinehas, *Hom.* 1 *Sam.* 1: 7 *Werke* 8. 13. 4ff. The special subtlety
lies in the fact that through the good Phinehas the succession after Eleazar,
the first "bishop", was continued, whereas the bad Phinehas came from Itha-
mar, 1 Chron. 24: 3; 1 Sam. 14: 3.
[3] Complaints, *Hom. Num.* 2: 1 *Werke* 7. 10. 6 ff.; cf. how in Ps. Clem., *Hom.*
3. 64 Lag. 54. 2 ff. "to be criticized by the crowd whom you will never satisfy",
is regarded as the hardest duty of the bishop.

position of the priesthood or the chair of a teacher, whereas a truly spiritual man, and one who is altogether free from secular considerations, . . . either holds an inferior position in the ministry or even remains among the multitude of the laity."[1] This fact continued to be Origen's chief difficulty with regard to the Apostolic succession, so that we find him countering his opponents' references to the validity of their orders with a characteristic reply. The bishops, so he said, used Matthew 16: 18–19 as an argument that to them, the successors of the Apostles, belonged the power of the keys. This, he replied, was true in so far as "they can show the works on account of which it has been said of that Peter, 'Thou art Peter, and upon this rock will I build my Church', that is, if the gates of hell shall not prevail against them."[2]

This remark owes its special significance not so much to the New Testament as to Jewish-Christian traditions. Since Origen was not inclined to attach too much importance to the historic St. Peter, it may be assumed that in this remark he did not see him in the light of the New Testament either. For there are no works of St. Peter mentioned in the Gospel—or even in the Acts—which would defeat the gates of hell, excepting his confession at Caesarea Philippi, and this was not what Origen had in mind. The pseudo-Clementines, however, made an attempt to close this imaginary gap; and it is suggested that Origen, being well acquainted with this literature, referred to the many miracles described there by which St. Peter defeated Simon Magus. Origen maintained that it was absurd that a great sinner, "only because he is addressed as bishop, should have the power to make those who are absolved by him to be absolved in heaven, and those who are bound by him to be bound in heaven".[3] This statement once more makes clear the issue between him and his opponents: was it tolerable that men who had bought their bishoprics should be endowed with that spiritual authority which was provided by their Apostolic succession? It is well known that in the history of the Church the mechanical theory of the

---

[1] Origen, *Hom.* 1 *Sam.* 1: 7 *Werke* 8. 9. 17 ff.
[2] Origen, *Comm. Matt.* 12: 14 *Werke* 10. 98. 18 ff.
[3] Origen, *ib.*, *Werke* 10. 99. 18.

Apostolic succession through the laying on of hands found its limit in the crime of "simony". It is remarkable therefore that Origen should already have been led to similar conclusions by means of the legend surrounding the conflict between Simon Peter and Simon Magus.

If, therefore, the effectiveness of the Apostolic succession was governed by certain moral prerequisites, it seems that Origen extended this limitation to all who possessed sacerdotal dignity. It has to be noticed that the description "bishops and presbyters" was applied not only to the unsatisfactory elements who were appointed, but also to the persons who made these appointments. If the participation of presbyters in the consecration of the bishops had been a recent abuse Origen would probably have remarked upon it; but he did not attack along this line. Although he expressly mentioned the appointment of bishops along with the ordination of the presbyters, he passed no remarks concerning the formal validity of either of these two rites. His criticism was directed solely against the effectiveness of both. Gross mismanagement in the selection of suitable persons made it inevitable that the clergy should not carry out their functions according to the demands of their sacred office, even though they had been validly appointed. If, therefore, Origen mentioned bishops and presbyters as being jointly responsible for this most unsatisfactory state of affairs, it appears that a rule comparable to the canon of Hippolytus (which has been cited at the beginning of this chapter) was already in existence in his time. The so-called "reform" in the consecration ceremonies of Heraclas was probably no more than the natural consequence of the consecration of Egyptian bishops by Demetrius.

The question thus arises whether the Alexandrian presbyterate ought to be regarded as a community of bishops. It is, however, difficult to accept this suggestion. First of all, Origen himself, who had been ordained presbyter in the Church of Palestine, claimed the same prerogative which they enjoyed, and this claim was supported by Pamphilus in the preface of his apology for Origen. This fact, if it be admitted that Origen was not just being untoward, sheds a new light upon the position of the presbyters at oriental synods; we may cite as instances that of Malchion at the second (third?) synod of Antioch, and, perhaps even that of Athanasius, the deacon, at Nicaea. Origen's contention, that the *charisma* of the Holy Spirit was the common basis for the Apostolic succession of bishops and presbyters, would find its natural expression in the part which these men played. This contention is, of course, a principle held by all who subscribe to the doctrine of the Apostolic succession. There was, however, a difference of emphasis. Origen seems to have held that the grave defects in the selection of bishops and clergy might interrupt the Apostolic succession, not because of any faults in the ritual, but because of the absence of those qualifications which are the fruits of the Spirit. By holding these views Origen stood at the cross-roads, at that position, where earlier gnostic convictions were linked up with those tendencies which eventually led to the Novatianist and Donatist schisms which claimed that only impeccable ministers were capable of administering the blessed Sacraments. Although Origen himself attempted a compromise by accepting his ordination as presbyter at the hands of a bishop, it is clear that he saw himself as a gnostic who was superior to any institutional ministry. However, having accepted the presbyterate within the earthly Church, he demanded that the moral standards of the ministry should be similar to the perfection of the true gnostic.

Origen's doctrine of the priesthood centred in the ministry of the Word. That was to be served with a self-denial, similar to that of Christ when He washed the feet of His disciples at the Last Supper.[1] Any self-sacrifice less complete was insufficient, and Origen's criticisms were all the more damning because he had put the standard so very high. The priesthood was granted to bishops and presbyters alike,[2] but it is wrong to draw the conclusion of K. Mueller that, for this

[1] Washing of feet, *Hom. Is.* 6: 3 *Werke* 8. 272. 19 ff.; *Comm. Rom.* 8: 4 Lo. 7. 214. K. Mueller, *Z.N.W.* 28 (1929), 285 n.; 292, referring to *Comm. Cant.* 2 *Werke* 8. 120. 10 ff., another relevant passage, where the bishop and his presbyters, sitting in the chancel, are contrasted with the deacons, has unfortunately built rather daring conclusions upon this slight foundation.

[2] Priesthood of presbyters, *Hom. Jer.* 12: 3 *Werke* 3. 89. 21 ff. K. Mueller, *op. cit.*

reason, the difference between the two was thought of as insignificant. As a presbyter Origen demanded that presbyters should submit to the bishop in the same way in which Jesus Himself had submitted to His earthly father according to Luke 2: 51, "and He went down with them to Nazareth and was subject unto them." This example was capable of silencing all excuses based upon intellectual superiority; "for," he said, "how should not I be subject unto the bishop, who has been appointed by God to be my father?"[1] Bishops had to be honoured as bishops, presbyters as presbyters, deacons as deacons, etc., each one in the rank accorded to him by the order of the Church, just as it should also be in the natural order of the family.[2] Nevertheless, the whole fabric of the Church rested upon the bishops: "the beams of the house are of cedar", Cant. 1: 17, allegorically signified to Origen the spiritual ministry of the bishops; "and the rafters fir" was the more modest allegory employed for presbyters.[3] It is also permissible to combine in this connexion two closely related remarks, although they were made with different intentions: the first, "it is reasonable to call the priests of the Church, because they are known as *speculatores*——a Latin attempt to express the twofold meaning of the Greek *episcopos*——the eyes of the Church, but the deacons and other ministers its hands"; the second, "I who appear to you as the right hand of God, being called a presbyter, and charged with the preaching of God's Word."[4] True, the first remark does not mention the presbyters, and it may be held that, possessing the priesthood, they are to be numbered among "the eyes" of the Church; but the second quotation shows that this conclusion would be somewhat precarious. In any case, if Origen openly brought charges against the bishops of his time, he did so because he had a real respect for the ministry of the bishop. The first remark is an interpretation of the Lord's command "pluck it out and cast it from thee", for

---

[1] Subjection to the bishop, *Hom. Luk.* 20 *Werke* 9. 133. 17 ff., where Origen also enjoined obedience to the presbyters.

[2] Origen, *Hom. Jer.* 14: 4 *Werke* 3. 108. 23 ff.

[3] Origen, *Comm. Cant.* 3 *Werke* 8. 177. 11 ff.

[4] Eyes of the Church, *Hom. Matt.* 13: 24 *Werke* 10. 246. 25 ff. Right hand, *Hom. Jos.* 7: 6 *Werke* 7. 334. 11 ff.

Origen held that every minister was liable to be removed from his office if proved to be unworthy of his vocation, with great shame to himself.[1] Certain obligations, in particular monogamy, were shared by all the four orders of the traditional ministry, bishops, presbyters, deacons, and widows, "who are also worthy of ecclesiastical honour"; . . . "but it is the bishop's duty which is the heaviest, demanded by the Saviour of the whole Church, and exacted in judgment, if it is not discharged."[2]

Origen thus confronts the student of Church history with a great though familiar difficulty. For, although he is our earliest available source for the local development of the doctrine of the Apostolic succession at Alexandria, he treats it very largely as a matter of course. He mainly discusses the borderline problems, as for instance the influence of "simony" upon the continuity of the Apostolic succession, or the Apostolic succession of other Church orders, including that of the teachers. He therefore creates a wrong impression upon scholars who are not aware of his tacit assumption of this succession or refuse to take it into account. From his allusions and hints there appear, however, the elements of a system which is different from its Western counterpart. On the one hand, there is the succession of the teachers in which pagan influences abound; on the other, there is the episcopal succession which is modelled mainly upon the Rabbinic and Jewish-Christian pattern. The great prominence given to the example of Moses and Joshua, a prominence which was much less emphasized by Irenaeus, suggests that the Western scheme had to pay less respect to Jewish-Christian conceptions than did Origen. Harnack's idea that pagan philosophical and religious influences played

---

[1] Origen, *Hom. Ez.* 10: 1 *Werke* 8. 417. 12 ff., a passage which also says, *et frequenter ab hominibus revocantur in pristinum gradum*—by way of a re-ordination? A. Harnack, *Kirchenverf.* 69 n. 1, is unhelpful. The remark about the reappointment is at any rate meant as a consolation for those who suffered such a humiliation.

[2] Fourfold ministry; monogamy, *Hom. Luk.* 17 fin. *Werke* 9. 120. 22 ff.; widows, *Hom. Is.* 6: 3 *Werke* 8. 273. 9 ff., cf. on the *diaconia* of women in general *Comm. Rom.* 10: 17 Lo. 7. 429, and Harnack *T.U.* 42. 4 (1919), 140 n. 1, who is correct with regard to the virgins, but wrong with regard to the widows. Pre-eminence of the bishops, *Orat.* 28. 4.

an important part in the formation of Origen's theory of the priesthood cannot be substantiated.[1]

Apostolicity was for Origen a quality characteristic of episcopacy rather than of the episcopate. He constantly challenged the bishops with a violence in the light of which even the most damaging indictments and recriminations appeared as a matter of course. To a large extent these were caused by his conflict with two successive bishops of Alexandria, and have to be judged in that context. However, the institution of episcopacy as such was represented by Origen as being endowed with the judicial power and rulership which had been accorded to St. Peter by the Lord at Caesarea Philippi. Methods of election were discussed by Origen only in so far as he demanded the popular vote and criticized it at the same time. The consecration of the bishops is nowhere explicitly dealt with by Origen; but from his casual remarks several probable conclusions may be derived. First, that the rite contained the laying on of hands, the characteristic of the consecration of Joshua, to which he repeatedly referred. Secondly, that presbyters were admitted along with the bishops to perform this rite, because they shared the priesthood with the bishops, although the bishops were granted a spiritual seniority. The main task of the priesthood was the ministry of the Word. So far Origen's thesis is quite clear, but in other respects it is somewhat obscured by later alterations. They were caused, on the one hand, by his over-emphasis on the succession of the teachers, and on the other hand by the uncertainty in his theological system of the lines of demarcation between the earthly Church, the Church of the

---

[1] A. Harnack, *Kirchenverf.* 78 n. 1; 84, suggests that the Christian conception of the priesthood was predominantly pagan. The only argument of his which carries some conviction is his reference to the priests among the Gnostic Marcians, because it is difficult to derive a priesthood among a sect which rejected the Old Testament, from the ancient Israelite priesthood. However, in view of the fact that there were also bishops of the Marcosii, Hippol., *Philos.* 6. 41. 4 ff., and presbyters among the Marcionites, Euseb., *H.E.* 4. 15. 46, it is more likely that the priesthood of the heretics was no more than an imitation of Catholic institutions. The pagan model is referred to by Tertullian, *ad Ux.*1. 6, and elsewhere and—strangely enough—in *Const. Apost.* 2. 28. 9, but Origen's only contribution to the matter is the remark about the Christian ascetics in *adv. Cels.* 7. 48.

angels, and the Church within man's soul. Here indeed are reasons to suspect heresy. None the less, it seems probable that the great respect which was paid to the ministry rather than to the ministers in eastern Christendom, and which continues even to this day, may well be due to developments which were first inaugurated by Origen.

One last remark may be added. In all his work Origen never treated of the episcopate of St. James. It may, therefore, be concluded that Eusebius, who in many respects depended upon Origen, when he placed the name of St. James at the head of his episcopal lists was drawing upon traditions which were earlier than Origen. In this way the silence of Origen seems to add an important feature to his testimony.

\* \* \* \* \*

These then are the results of our survey of the earliest sources mentioning the Apostolic succession. First, that they do not connect with the attempts made especially in the Pastoral Epistles to establish such a succession, but have their origin elsewhere. Secondly, that the type of the early succession lists is the same at Jerusalem, Rome, Antioch, and Alexandria, and closely resembles the type of the various lists of the succession of the Jewish High Priests. The adoption of this type was influenced by the Jewish doctrine that the *Christos hegoumenos* was the succession of the Jewish High Priests; and, as we have seen, a special Christian interest in the succession of the High Priests is noticeable in the Chronicle of Hippolytus. Thirdly, that all the earliest references to the Apostolic succession come from Jewish-Christian sources—I *Clement*, the pseudo-Clementines, and Hegesippus; and that they exhibit a competition between St. James, the brother of the Lord, and St. Peter for the first place, a competition decided in favour of St. James in the Canon of Eusebius-Jerome. Fourthly, that there were other types of succession within the Christian Church, especially that of the Christian prophets in Asia Minor, which was also modelled upon a Jewish pattern. This prophetic succession was forcibly brought to an end because

of the Montanist troubles, but it left its impress upon the
doctrine of the Apostolic succession. Less prominent was
the conception of a succession of Christian teachers, which
may have been partly dependent upon pagan models.

Out of these various and somewhat disparate elements
Irenaeus created the doctrine of the Apostolic succession,
which was further developed by his pupils Hippolytus and
Tertullian. At Alexandria the peculiar conditions obtaining
there caused Origen to insist upon the fact that "simony"
invalidated the orders of a man, even if he had been duly
consecrated bishop. Both Irenaeus and Origen held that
the Apostolic succession cannot be detached from the
Apostolic tradition, because the first—and for Origen the
most important—duty of Christian priests is the ministry of
the Word.

# *Index of Sources*
## BIBLICAL

# NON-BIBLICAL

# General Index

Aaron, 73
 house of, 44, 45, 50
Abimelech, 143
Abomination, 58 f.
Abraham, 143
Acts, apocryphal, 61, 71 f.
 of martyrs, 41, 85 and n. 1
 of Paul, 71, 97
 of Perpetua, 93
 of Peter, 74, 118
 of Polycarp, 41, 95 n. 1
 of the Apostles, 21, 68, 75
Aelia, 40
Africanus, 35 f., 39, 40, 54, 59, 135
Agabus, 30, 69, 85
Ahijah of Shilo, 17
Alcimus, 44, 49 f., 51 f., 59
Alexander Jannaeus, 44, 53, 55, 57 f.,
 59, 79
 of Jerusalem, 40 n. 2
 of Lyons, 100
Alexandria, 36, 37, 39, 40, 62, 63, 79,
 81, 132, 143, 149, 156, 158
Alogoi, 94
Ambition, 144, 146
Ammia of Philadelphia, 69, 88, 94
Ananias, 12, 24
Andronicus, 13
Angels, 79, 107, 137, 139 f.
Anno Domini, 41 f., 51, 60
Antigonus of Socho, 46
Antioch, 23, 24, 25 f., 29, 34, 36, 37,
 39, 40, 62, 71, 74 f., 77, 80,
 85, 95, 111, 137, 146, 148,
 154, 158
 in Pisidia, 26, 34
Antiochus Epiphanes, 47, 49, 58
Apocalypse, 80, 91 f., 93, 94
Apollos, 25
Apophthegmata, 85
*apostellein*, 19
Apostle, 12, 13, 14 f., 19 f., 29, 33,
 65, 66, 68, 70, 77, 79 f., 84, 86,
 89 n. 2, 96, 97, 110, 122, 127 f.,
 136 f., 139, 146, 150, 152
Apostolic, 13, 20 f., 36, 94, 108, 109,
 119 f., 125, 157
*apostolos*, 16 and n. 3, 17 n. 1, 18 f.,
 19 n. 3., 70 n. 1, 78
Appointment of ministers, 35
Aquila, 25
Archippus, 24
*archontes*, 27, 73 f., 73 n. 4, 112, 150
Aristeas, letter of, 45
Aristion, 112, 116

Aristobulus, 52 f., 57 f., 79
Artaxerxes I, 54, 56, 57
Ascetics, 140 f., 157 n. 1
Attorney, power of, 17 f., 19
Augustine of Hippo, 131

Babylon, 49, 53 f., 57 f., 61, 76
Baptism, 14, 24, 26, 31, 69, 86 n. 1,
 96, 128, 133
Barnabas, 23, 25 f., 29, 32 f., 34, 85,
 102
Basil the Great, 138
Basilides, 108
Biographies of Saints, 99
Bishop, 11, 12, 14, 26, 28, 30, 34, 59,
 66, 69, 77, 79, 82 and n. 1, 83, 84,
 90, 94, 95, 96, 98, 107, 112, 114,
 120, 128, 129, 137 f., 140, 145, 146,
 147, 148 f., 150, 151, 153, 154 f.
Bishopric, 144, 152

Caesarea Philippi, 25, 152, 157
Calendar, civil, 41, 60
Callistus, 55, 73, 114, 128, 143, 146
Canon, apostolic, 20, 94, 95, 108,
 109, 112
Canon law, 103 f.
Canon Muratori, 109, 112, 118
Canon of Eusebius, 35 ff., 39, 43 f.,
 53 f., 55 f., 62, 67 f., 72, 81, 135,
 137 n. 2
Canones Hippolyti, 134
Careerism, 146
Carthage, 95, 148
Catechetical school of Alexandria,
 135 f., 142, 144, 150 n. 5
*cathedra*, 73, 82, 90, 148 f.
Celsus, 85 n. 2, 92, 141
*character indelebilis*, 113 f., 156
*charisma*, 32, 70, 90, 99 f., 113, 114,
 120, 125, 136, 154
*cheirotonein*, 16
*Christos hegoumenos*, 56 ff., 76, 158
Chronicle, Armenian, 36
 of Africanus, 36, 39, 56, 86
 of Hippolytus, 36, 47, 56, 86, 88
Chronicon paschale, 53
Church, African, 128, 130 f.
 among the Gentiles, 24, 27 f.,
  29, 35, 65, 68, 80
 Apostolic, 20
 Catholic, 30, 64, 82, 83, 84, 89,
  94, 99, 107, 109, 132, 136
 —constitution, 21, 75, 83, 89, 130

# General Index

Church, earthly—heavenly, 139, 140, 141, 157 f.
heavenly, 82
in Asia Minor, 63, 66, 69, 70 f., 81, 117
in Gaul, 130
in Judaea, 23, 30
of the circumcision, 25, 63 f., 68, 81 f.
Clement of Alexandria, 40, 79, 98, 104, 111, 112, 133 ff., 139, 144 f.
of Rome, 72, 76, 77 f., 80, 81, 119
Ps.-Clement, 71 n. 1, 71 ff., 81 f., 89
Codex Bezae, 23 n. 1, 28 f., 34, 35, 82
Colossae, 24
Consecration, 12, 106, 119, 121, 133 f., 153, 157
Corinth, 36, 63
Corruption, 145, 147
Council of the Apostles, 23, 28, 105
Creed, 20, 95, 109, 112, 127
Crescens, 76
Cyprian, 67, 99, 132, 148
Ps.-Cyprian, 124
Cyrus, 54

Damascus, 24, 84
Daniel, 52, 53, 54, 58 f., 60 f.
Darius, 55, 57
David, 44
kingdom of, 25
Deacon, 11, 12, 27, 77, 83, 84, 96, 98, 129, 139, 144, 145, 146, 147, 151, 154 n. 1
Demetrius of Alexandria, 40, 118, 135, 136 n. 1, 153
Derbe, 26, 34
diadoche, 33, 138
Didache, 70, 76, 85 n. 2, 89, 90, 92, 96, 98
Didascalia, 107
Diogenes Laertius, 43, 115
Dionysius of Alexandria, 57
Exiguus, 41
the Areopagite, 67
Discerning of spirits, 91 f.
Disciple, 24
Divorce, 20
Doctor Ecclesiae, 150
Doctrina Addai, 66 f., 118
Domitian, 64
Domnus of Antioch, 148
Donatists, 131, 154
dux et doctor, 140

Ebion, 136
Edessa, 66, 95, 119
Elders, Christian, 28 f., 29 n. 1
Jewish, 27, 44
Eleazar, 45, 150, 151

Eli, 151
Elijah, 88
Eminent men, 70, 77, 96
engrapha, 38 f.
entolai, 29
Epaphras, 24
Ephesus, 26, 31, 67, 76 n. 2, 91, 119, 128
Episcopacy, 11, 83, 91, 116, 125, 135, 157
episcopus, 28, 65, 112, 113, 117, 121, 130, 150, 155
episcoporum, 73
Epistle to the Hebrews, 80
Epistles, Pastoral, 21, 26 ff., 34, 67, 72, 82, 129 f., 158
Eschatology, 42, 52, 60
Euodius of Antioch, 137
Eusebius, 30, 31, 35 f., 39, 40, 41, 42, 48, 51, 53, 55, 59, 68, 111, 115, 135
Evangelists, 70, 84, 96
Eve, 18 n. 2
Excerpta Barbari, 53, 55 f.
Eyes of the Church, 155
Ezekiah, High Priest, 45
Ezra, 55

Fila regnorum, 38, 39, 42
Florinus, 111

Gaius of Jerusalem, 40 n. 1
Glaucias, 108
Gnosticism, 30 n. 1, 108, 123, 127, 132, 135
Gnostics, Catholic, 83, 98, 104, 134 f., 138 f., 142
Gregory of Nyssa, 138

Hadrian, 38, 40, 59 f., 63, 70 n. 2, 75, 108
Hasidean Order, 52 n. 1
Hasmonaeans, 44, 47, 48, 51
Hebrews, 22
Ps.-Hecataeus, 45
Hegesippus, 36, 39 f., 41, 62, 63 f., 81, 92, 107, 117 n. 5, 118, 122, 123, 137
Ps.-Hegesippus, 57 f., 60
hegoumenoi, 89
Hellenists, 22
Heraclas, 133, 135 f., 136 n. 1, 153
Heretics, 112, 127, 157 n. 1
Hermas, 77, 78, 85 n. 2, 87, 90, 92, 93, 112, 146
Herod the Great, 43 n. 1, 48, 52, 53, 59, 61, 75
Hierarchy, 83, 99
High Pontiff, 146
High Priest, 14 f., 35 f., 39, 56 f., 59 ff., 73, 82, 91, 92, 95, 98, 107,

113, 119, 121, 124 ff., 132, 134, 140, 143
Holy Spirit, 23, 30, 32, 34, 71, 84 ff., 88, 96, 99, 102, 104, 106, 124, 139, 140
Hospitality, 137

Iconium, 26, 34
Ignatius of Antioch, 72, 74, 76 f., 77 n. 1, 100, 111, 137
Infallibility, 89 and n. 3, 91, 95, 108
Inscriptions of Venosa, 16 n. 2
Irenaeus, 38, 40 f., 62, 72, 81, 91, 107 ff., 137, 138, 156

James of Jerusalem, 13, 14, 21, 23, 28 f., 35, 39, 40, 64 f., 65 n. 4, 67 f., 72, 73 f., 77, 79 ff., 107 f., 158
James of Zebedee, 13, 22, 23, 24
Jason, High Priest, 44, 59
Jason of Cyrene, 51, 52, 53, 59
Jeroboam, 146
Jerome, 17, 23 n. 1, 29, 35, 37, 40, 53, 133, 134
Jerusalem, bishops of, 38 f., 41, 59, 60 f., 62, 75
Church at, 13, 21, 23, 25, 26 ff., 29 f., 34, 35, 37, 38, 63, 66, 72, 81 f., 122, 158
destruction of, 75
temple at, 51, 55, 58 f.
Jeshua, High Priest, 54 f., 57
John, Apostle, 22, 23, 25, 28, 31, 91, 94, 107, 108, 110, 111, 112, 128
Mark, 26, 127
presbyter, 112, 116
the Baptist, 31, 54, 76, 88, 126
Jonathan Maccabaeus, 49 f.
Joseph Justus, 21
Josephus, 30, 42, 45, 48 f., 51, 53, 58
Joshua, 31 f., 44, 87, 147, 149, 150 f., 156
Judas, brother of James, 22, 31, 146, 147
Iscariot, 22, 31, 146, 147
the prophet, 26, 69
Julianus of Jerusalem, 40 n. 2
Junia, 13
Justin Martyr, 75, 81, 88, 112
Justus of Jerusalem, 40, 64

Kings, 52, 121 n. 1
Jewish, 86
Kingship, 78

Law, Mosaic, 25, 30, 63, 75 f., 104 f., 122
Laying on of hands, 13, 15, 16, 22, 31, 32, 33, 82, 88, 102, 106, 125 f., 133, 149, 153, 157

*Leitourgia*, 77
Leprosy, 150
Levites, 15, 31 f., 78, 120, 151
Liberian catalogue, 38
*Libri generationis*, 57 n. 1
Linus, 67
List of Samaritan gnostics, 123
Lists of annual magistrates, 43
of episcopal succession, 35 ff., 44 ff., 51, 59 f., 68, 72, 107, 128
of high priests, 42 f., 48 ff., 53 ff., 55, 56, 58, 59 f., 72, 76, 107
of philosophers, 43, 46
of prophets, 43, 44, 47, 76
of rabbis, 43, 44, 46
of royal succession, 38, 42 f., 48 ff.
of succession, Jewish, 44, 46
Logos, 86, 93, 114
Lucian of Samosata, 85 n. 2, 92
Lucius of Cyrene, 26
Luke, 23, 28, 33
Luther, Martin, 97
Lystra, 26, 34

Maccabees, 45
Macrocosm, 141
*magisterium*, 123, 124
Mal'ak, 107
Malachi, 88
Manichees, 68
Marcion, 89, 108, 127, 136
Martyrs, 83, 92, 95, 100, 136 n. 3, 140
*mathetria*, 18
Mattathias, 44
Matthias, 11, 21 f., 30, 108, 149
Maximilla, 70
Maximin Daia, 56
Melchisedec, 78
Melito, 90
Menelaus, High Priest, 44, 50
Messiah, 53, 54 f., 60
Michael, 107 n. 3
Millennium, 110, 115 f.
Ministry, Apostolic, 20 f., 46, 84, 86, 92, 95
charismatic, 83, 99 ff.
dependent, 12, 14
essential, 13, 14
—dependent, 11
institutional, 100 f., 104, 132, 134, 142, 144, 154
local, 89 f.
of the Word, 12, 15, 98, 123, 128, 140, 150, 154, 157
prophetic, 30, 84 f., 85 n. 1, 86 f., 90 ff., 94, 99, 108, 126
sacerdotal, 11, 15, 107, 129
spiritual, 98
threefold, 11, 83
transitional, 83 f., 95
Missionaries, 13, 24, 34, 70 f., 84, 96

CPSIA information can be obtained
at www.ICGtesting.com
Printed in the USA
LVHW082130030721
691852LV00010B/491